The MAKING of a WRITER

The MAKING of a WRITER

A Christian Writer's Guide

SHERWOOD ELIOT WIRT

AUGSBURG Publishing House • Minneapolis

THE MAKING OF A WRITER
A Christian Writer's Guide

Copyright © 1987 Sherwood Eliot Wirt

All rights reserved. Except for brief quotations in critical articles or reviews, no part of this book may be reproduced in any manner without prior written permission from the publisher. Write to: Permissions, Augsburg Publishing House, 426 S. Fifth St., Box 1209, Minneapolis MN 55440.

Scripture quotations unless otherwise noted are from the Holy Bible: New International Version. Copyright 1978 by the New York International Bible Society. Used by permission of Zondervan Bible Publishers.

Library of Congress Cataloging-in-Publication Data

Wirt, Sherwood Eliot.
  THE MAKING OF A WRITER.

  Bibliography: p.
  1. Christian literature—Authorship.   I. Title.
  BR117.W57   1987   808'.0662   87-1099
  ISBN 0-8066-2269-5

Manufactured in the U.S.A.   APH 10-4263

1   2   3   4   5   6   7   8   9   0   1   2   3   4   5   6   7   8   9

*To the Critiquers
of the San Diego County
Christian Writers' Guild*

CONTENTS

Preface	9
1. The Pursuit of Excellence	13
2. Starting with the Right Attitude	19
3. Beginning to Think Professionally	28
4. The World of a Writer	38
5. Four Keys to Successful Writing	46
6. What the Readers Want	58
7. Putting in the Sparkle	65
8. The Significance of Words	71
9. The Effective Use of Words	78
10. The Light Touch	84
11. The Strong Touch	91
12. The Writer and the Bible	98
13. The Writer As Editor	106
14. The Excitement of Fiction	114
15. Go after the Interview	128
16. The Critique Group	137
17. The Bright Side of Rejections	143
18. What the Editors Want	152
Notes	158
Appendix: Tools for the Professional Christian Writer	159

PREFACE

Christian writers today face the most favorable opportunity offered them since the invention of printing. Each week a million new persons are learning how to read. Every few days a new Christian bookstore opens. The demand for Christian writing of quality far exceeds the supply. Meanwhile the human race is experiencing a depletion of worthwhile literature; people are famished for righteousness in print. Millions of men, women, and young people long for good words, helpful and hopeful words, relevant words, Spirit-filled words of strength and assurance.

Where are the trained professional writers who will set forth the truth about good and evil in the idiom of our time? I believe they are everywhere. The purpose of this book is to find them, encourage them, and set them to work.

Because I spent a quarter of a century trying unsuccessfully to break into print, I have a particular interest in bridging the gulf between writers and editors. I now see that from a human standpoint, my long dry spell was quite unnecessary. The simple expedient of seeking advice from the right people can make all the difference to an aspiring writer. Therein lay part of my problem: I was not ready to seek advice, let alone heed it. The writer prepared to submit to the rules can have unlimited outreach, influence, and effectiveness in the spreading of God's Word through literature. God never neglects an available servant.

But writing is only a means to an end. My deepest concern is not for the writer but for the person who reads. What people read, they become. Every great movement to sweep through the human race has been brought about through writing. That the pen is mightier than the sword is not rhetoric; it is history.

Think of the reformation that took place in Israel under Josiah as the result of Hilkiah's discovery of a book in the temple. Think of Christianity itself, carried on the wings of Holy Scripture across the ancient world. The echo of Apollos' sermons long since died out in the hills of Asia Minor; we have no knowledge of the preaching of Philip that brought such great joy to Samaria; yet the sermons of Stephen, and Peter, and Paul have inspired the church for 2000 years, and if the Lord tarries, will inspire us for generations to come. Someone put them in writing!

The Reformation of the 16th century was first of all a literary activity. John Froben published Martin Luther's tracts in Wittenberg and circulated them all over Europe. Zwingli read them in Switzerland, Calvin in France, Cranmer in Britain, Ochino in Italy, Valdes in Spain—and the Reformation was under way.

Modern-day communism did not capture two-fifths of the earth's surface through tanks and missiles, but through the writings of Karl Marx, a journalist. Maoism took control of China not through the actions of the Red Guards, but by the mass distribution of Mao's "Little Red Book."

A minister said to me once, "Each Sunday I preach to about 100 people in my congregation. But every day I reach 3000 people through my front-page column in our daily newspaper."

Today's readers are exposed to an unprecedented clamor for their attention. Yet the time comes when the right piece of literature, placed in their hands, can effectively transform their behavior and character. They will take it home, read it, reflect quietly on their lives, and perhaps offer up a prayer to God. That is what God wants and expects of Christian literature and those who write it.

Much of the material in this volume has never before appeared in print. Some chapters first appeared in two of my earlier books: *You Can Tell the World* (Augsburg, 1975) and *Getting into Print* (Thomas Nelson, 1977). These chapters have been revised for this book, and some have been completely rewritten. For 20 years I have been lecturing on writing at seminars and conferences in 15 countries around the world, from Nome, Alaska, to Durban, South Africa. Those talks are in this book. I wish to thank the hundreds of people who have shared their expertise with me at these conferences. I especially would like to thank my former secretary, Ruth McKinney, now an author, for her contribution to Chapter 17.

And now to all who peruse these pages I add the word of encouragement from the psalmist: "The Lord announced the word, and great was the company of those who proclaimed it" (Ps. 68:11).

1

THE PURSUIT OF EXCELLENCE

In Christian literature we have the greatest subject in all history, the man from Nazareth. We have the greatest source of truth, the Bible; the greatest message of hope, eternal life; the greatest benefit to offer, salvation from sin; the greatest motivator to the good life, the gospel. More than that, Christianity has provided the world with its most thrilling music, has inspired the finest in architecture and art, and has stirred the sublimest passions and the noblest sacrifices in individuals.

Now in the late 20th century, when all this has been made available to us through the miracle of mass communication, I ask you, why shouldn't it evoke great writing from among us? What's holding us back from literary excellence?

I believe that God, who fashioned the galaxies with his supernatural sense of timing, has used that same sidereal timing to cause you to read this page and to put this question to you.

He is driving his scribes out of the temple, telling us we've been cogitating in there long enough. He wants us out in the middle of things like Amos and Jeremiah, discovering what's going on and writing about it. He wants us to take the lid off the Christian message. He wants us to write the love language of the 1980s and 1990s. He is showing us all the outlets—print, film, television, radio, cassettes, videocassettes, pulpit—ready to go to work for him. He wants us to use the media to make things happen.

"Proclaim this message . . . . Stand at the gate and proclaim . . . . Write in a book all the words I have spoken to you" (Jer. 3:12; 7:2; 30:2). Over and over the sacred Scriptures tell us to forget about ourselves and to start talking up God, to concentrate on objective truth. All the reasonings of men can lead us only to Hiroshima and Beirut, but in Christ lies the promise of peace.

We all know these things, or should; but as writers we are asking further, how do we communicate truth to our generation? What does it take, as we approach the year 2000, to achieve literary excellence or even come near it? *Genius?* Forget it. That quality was left out of our makeup. *Zeal?* Well, we have a little. *Vocabulary?* We're still having trouble with words like "egregious," "arcane," and "desideratum." *Fasting?* Let's see, when is coffee break? *Imagination? Brain power?* We pass.

Let's admit that we don't have it, and start from there. Let's say frankly that for us to compose a decent sentence takes blood, toil, tears, and sweat, and turning out a really sparkling page of copy means an enormous amount of rewriting.

Now at least we're on bedrock. Like the Pilgrim in the Slough of Despond, we have touched the bottom and found it to be sound.¹ The apostle Paul wrote some words to the Corinthians that we might adapt to our situation: "You see your calling, brothers and sisters, that not many talented are among us, not many gifted; not many giants or best-sellers; but God has chosen the hacks of the world to show up the literary elite, that *The New York Times* reviewers might not glory in his presence." But the apostle added that he was struggling together with us toward the mark of excellence (Phil. 3:14).

But when we speak of the pursuit of excellence, of going for the gold medal, we need to distinguish between great literature as the world acknowledges it and great Christian literature. In many respects the standards are the same, but there is one important difference. It is not the use of religious phrases or religious themes. The difference lies between merely descriptive writing and writing that motivates. Thomas de Quincey once named three categories: the literature of *irrelevance,* the literature of *knowledge,* and the literature of *power.* We all know about the literature of *irrelevance;* there is far too much of it in our Christian bookstores. There is also the literature of *knowledge,* whose function is to teach. It is basically cognitive, and appeals to the mind. But the literature of *power* is not just cognitive, it is causal; its function is to move. Thus we might call the horoscope column in the daily newspaper the literature of irrelevance; the discourses of Epictetus the literature of knowledge; but the *Communist Manifesto* and the epistle to the Galatians would be the literature of power.

It is not enough for the copy we turn out to wear a cross on its escutcheon, not enough that we maintain our orthodoxy and express ourselves clearly and earnestly. What we write has to do things to people, to motivate them. It has to be causal if it is to be great: "Put on the full armor of God.... Stand firm and do not let yourselves be burdened again by a yoke of slavery.... Go into all the world and preach the good news" (Eph. 6:11; Gal. 5:1; Mark 16:15). Martin Luther once wrote, "Oh, it is a living, creative, active, mighty thing, this faith."[2] That is the way to think of great Christian writing. It is more than beauty, more than entertainment, more than richness of style, even though it may contain all three. It is the literature of power.

So when we speak of the pursuit of excellence, we are not thinking of cleverness, brilliance, elegance, facility of expression, or even clarity of thought. Hemingway, Maugham, Mailer, and Pynchon wrote from motives different from ours. But having said that, we cannot ignore the rules of good writing or those who have mastered them. A true professional learns both from his peers and his competitors. Paul learned from Menander; Augustine learned from Virgil.

One can also learn from a good editor. Let me share with you a portion of a letter written to me by an editor after I had submitted a nonfiction book manuscript. These are the editor's words:

> There is one problem with your manuscript that overarches all others: the story is emotionally flat. There is no drama, no pathos, where there should be. I am not drawn along by the story at all, not caught up in the drama of this man's life. You have succeeded in talking to all the necessary people and getting the facts of the story straight, but you have not added to the factual account those storytelling elements that provide life and color, that reach the reader's emotions as well as his intellect. The result is that as I read the manuscript, I feel very much as though I am having a story told to me, as opposed to feeling I am reading a marvelous story. There is only the narrator telling

rather than showing what was going on. The story is always at arm's length; I never feel as though I am there. In short, I think you need to go through another draft of the manuscript. I realize I am asking a great deal of you, but I believe it is in the best interests of the book.

And there followed some technical suggestions.

As the words sank into my consciousness, and my skin began to crawl, I began to see myself as one of the great mediocre writers of the world. But I had recently read Tom Wolfe's book, *The Right Stuff,* and on an impulse I reread the description of John Glenn's feelings as he was coming into the atmosphere after his pioneer voyage in outer space. Many things might be said about Wolfe's writing, but he is not mediocre. He puts you in that capsule, and you watch the broken pieces of the heatshield come flying past your window, and you realize that you are about to be burned to a crisp. You are lost, lost in space, and a stranger to the earth.

Well, after that little ride, I went back to my Memorywriter with a vengeance. The biggest hurdle was my own laziness. Once over that, I had a clear vision of what needed to be done, and proceeded to do it. The book was published and has gone into a third printing.

In the writing of 20 books I have been taught many things about this fascinating field of writing: how to do it and how not to do it; how to tell a marketable idea from a poor one; how to make friends with editors and how to keep that friendship; how to strive for a style that pleases the reader; and most important, how the Holy Spirit can use literature to bring glory to God.

In working with different writers' groups I have learned what leads to professional competence and success, and what holds writers back. Many factors are involved in the making of a writer; some are spiritual, some physical, some psychological. In this book we shall limit ourselves to the craft itself, and the craftsman as such. We shall concentrate on the pursuit and achievement of excellence. To do that, we shall wade into the stream of history and swim alongside some of the writing men and women who have interpreted truth down through the ages and have passed the word to us. We shall become aware of the joy, the color, the music, the elixir, the mystique that goes with writing. We shall not talk about our lack of preparation, the mistakes we made in our studies, the books we haven't read. Forget all that. We're starting with now.

2

STARTING WITH THE RIGHT ATTITUDE

Many people who attend writing schools and writers' conferences leave discouraged. They arrived with the hope that something sensational would happen to them, something that would jolt them right into the profession, or into the higher circles thereof. At the very least they might find out what to do with the disorganized mess they were struggling with. At the most they would meet the dream editor, or unload their manuscript on some dream house, or be handed a dream assignment. They might even be offered a dream job.

As the writers' conference proceeds, the dreamers wake up. They fill pages of notebooks with admonitions about what to do and what not to do: "Don't leave coffee rings on your typing paper. . . .Don't telephone the editor collect. . . .Don't write during a full moon." They watch people parade across the platform, all smiling, all saying one way or another, "I did it!" It's too much! The dreamers are overwhelmed.

A man and his wife flew from Oklahoma to our school of writing in Minnesota. Shortly afterward my wife and I were driving through that state and we stopped in to visit. The man said to me, "I learned one thing up there: that writing is a lot of work. I'm not about to do it." The curious fact is that this man is not lazy; he has memorized more Scripture than anyone I know, and he has done it in several versions.

But I will grant his premise: writing is work. So is everything else that is worthwhile. But writing is also joy. (I am not talking about joy over a royalty check. That is another matter and if it becomes too important, it can kill the joy you have in writing.) Most craftsmen find an inner joy in working at their craft, exercising skills, doing what they are good at. The writer is not different.

Historians tell us that Michelangelo became discouraged lying on his back year after year, painting the ceiling of the Sistine Chapel. I am sure David must have had some times of testing when he was putting together Psalm 23. Paul must have been terribly depressed by the conditions in that prison in Rome when he was trying to compose a letter to the church in Colossae.

But what does James tell us to do? "Consider it pure joy" (James 1:2). And if you ask athletes, they will tell you they derive pleasure from lifting weights and performing backward somersaults. There is pleasure in sport as there is pleasure in the performing arts. And there is pleasure in writing, not just in the honors that may or may not come, but in the actual execution of the writing itself. Give me food and sleep and exercise, and put me in a room by myself with an electric typewriter, a Bible, some dictionaries, a synonym-finder, and an idea, and for three hours I wouldn't trade places with anyone on earth.

Bruce Jenner, the Olympic champion, said after stepping down from the victory stand in Montreal, "There's no place left to climb." Writers never say that, because their best work always lies just ahead. Which would you rather have, a flight bag full of medals that tarnish or a published piece that will bring inspiration and hope to other people and perhaps draw them closer to God?

When you chop your own wood, they say, it warms you twice. It is the same with a Christian writer. The writer is blessed twice: while working on the piece and when people read it and respond to it. Augustine wrote his *Confessions* in his early 40s, at a time when athletes are through with competition. By the time Augustine died 30 years later, the *Confessions* had already become a classic and was being read by Christians all over the Mediterranean world. He had joy in the writing and joy in the effect his writing had on others. (I don't know what his royalty checks were.)

There are no shortcuts to craftsmanship in any endeavor, but let me suggest some ways in which we writers can reduce the hard routine of composition to a minimum and thereby increase our personal enjoyment of it.

First, let's make sure our tools are sharp. Clean keys, fresh ribbon, new paper, good lighting, even temperature, neat surroundings—all help to create a climate of contentment. Distractions should be kept to a minimum. Background music is fine for washing dishes, but not for writing. You need to concentrate, and good working conditions are essential.

And yet distractions and interruptions do come in spite of everything. The important thing is not to let them annoy us, but to maintain our Christian love and equilibrium. Two of the world's masterpieces of literature, *Pilgrim's Progress* and *Don Quixote*, were written partly in prison in an environment where, to use Cervantes' words, "Every annoyance has its home and every mournful sound its habitation."

Second, let's have our facts ready. If we have covered the ground, amassed our material, and done our homework, then the writing becomes a game with words. When I was a chaplain in the United States Air Force, I was told never to call on my commanding officer until I had all my facts together. In the same way, never sit down at your machine until you have your facts. The amateur starts with half-formed ideas and pops off about something not thoroughly researched. The professional waits until he or she has touched all the bases, has made those phone calls or gone to the library and checked out that one point.

After we have it all together alongside our machine, the only thing that concerns us is, How can I say what I want to say in a way that will make the world, the readership, sit up and take notice? How can I make my point strongly without distorting it? It is a problem each of us has to work out, but the synonym finder or thesaurus will help by providing us with words that are appropriate and well chosen. Notice, the hard work was the leg work, not the writing. The writing is the craft, and the writer enjoys it.

Third, bite the bullet of responsibility. One of the great lines of Scripture tells of Jesus, "who for the joy set before him endured the cross, scorning its shame and sat down at the right hand of the throne of God" (Heb. 12:2). Joy in going to the cross! It was the same kind of joy James was talking about when he said, "Consider it pure joy." And he is really talking about joy, not a put-on. If we have something to say about Jesus Christ, let's say it firmly, clearly, strongly, but with joy. Let's not circle around; let's not evade; let's not mince. Let's not "woffle," as the Scots say. It is our duty to say it; it is our responsibility to witness to Jesus Christ. Let's do it with joy.

Fourth, write as a free person. Remember what Jesus said: "If the Son sets you free, you will be free indeed" (John 8:36). That means we are really free; we do not have to stay with one kind of writing. Charles Lutwidge Dodgson was a mathematician; he wrote books in his field, but he also wrote *Alice in Wonderland* under his pseudonym Lewis Carroll. Within the framework of Christian responsibility we can let go and be as versatile as we like.

We may write history as fiction, or fiction as history. We may be as suave in our writing as Malcolm Muggeridge, or as primitive as the early Nicky Cruz.

We may write comedy or tragedy, contemporary history or allegory. We may use simile and metaphor. We may whip out a paperback testimony or grind out a theology of the Old Testament. We are free! We can write anything we wish. If we prefer to write about Jesus indirectly, as C. S. Lewis did in the Chronicles of Narnia, that is our privilege; or we can drop Jesus into every paragraph. We may write doggerel verses and set them to guitar music, or we may compose a heroic epic about the pageantry of Christendom suitable for an oratorio. We are free—free in Christ.

Fifth, be filled with the Spirit. When Jesus warned his disciples that they would have to give their testimony before magistrates and governors, he said, "Do not worry about how you will defend yourselves or what you will say, for the Holy

Spirit will teach you at that time what you should say" (Luke 12:11-12).

I cannot explain fully what it means to be filled with the Spirit at this time; I have sought to do that in my little book *Afterglow*. But I will say this: when we write in the Spirit, the Spirit of God takes care of our responsibility to witness; he witnesses with our spirit through our writing.

When you attend a writers' conference, remember that the rules you get from the faculty are not really rules; they are guidelines. The Christian writer writes not by law but by grace. You may fool everyone by going your own way and writing a best-seller. It has been done more than once.

Jesus Christ has a claim on us; he wants us to write for him, and he wants us to enjoy our writing. In the year 1957 in a minister's study in Oakland, California, sat a very disheartened writer. He had been hitting the typewriter for 25 years, and was right back where he started. In his files were three full-length book manuscripts plastered with rejection slips. He had also written dozens of unpublished short stories, articles, interviews, half-finished essays, and gobs of poetry. That writer was I.

When the dam finally broke, it was the Lord who broke it. It was as if he said, "Forget about your problems. Forget about everything you have written. I am the Lord your God. Write about me." Well, my first book was about Jesus' Beatitudes. A later book was about the Holy Spirit. A third book was about the Psalms. I had so much joy writing those books, I wish I could write them all over again.

Sixth, make use of God's shelf. You have never heard of God's shelf? Peter knew about it. John Mark knew about it. David knew about it. Hannah Whitall Smith tells us something about it in her book *The Christian's Secret of a Happy*

STARTING WITH THE RIGHT ATTITUDE   25

Life. She describes the shelf in her imagery of the Potter and the clay. She says that sometimes the Potter takes the clay he is working with and lays it on the shelf and leaves it and goes on to work with something else. Then after a while he takes it down and works with it some more.

The piece you are working on that has been giving you so much trouble that the joy has gone out of it—why not put it on the shelf for a few days or weeks? And in the meantime, insert a fresh sheet of paper in your typewriter and begin to write about what God is doing now in your life. Relate something that has recently happened to you or someone else, or write about something in your church.

You say, "No one will be interested in me." Well, I'm interested in you. I would like to see your story in written form. And don't tell me writing about yourself is drudgery! I won't believe it; I know better. Yes, it is work, but it is also an adventure. Take that experience of yours and use some of your expertise to sift and shape it. Make it professional. Describe it with smoothness and with suspense.

We don't have to make a big production of our past. Certain standards of modesty prevail in Christian writing. At the same time we have to be realistic. Balance modesty and realism in your mind and give us the result. Remember, when you describe what happened in the past, you look back from a perspective you didn't have then. In his *Confessions* Augustine looked over his life, but every time he described some peccadillo, he was telling it to the Lord, and the struggle was evident.

The professional writer can make his or her testimony sound acceptable and yet realistic and interesting. Let us see the forces that were playing on you, that brought you to your present state of Christian maturity as God has dealt with you. It makes good copy.

If you are disheartened about your writing, try writing about the Lord and see if the Holy Spirit will not use it. See if you don't get a lift; the darkness begins to dissipate and the sun breaks through and you begin to praise God with joy.

Seventh, and finally, you will find joy in your writing if you put joy into it. Ladle it in. Your stuff doesn't have to sound dreary. Mix it with humor. Humor is acceptable, especially when directed at oneself. It's easy to get a laugh by poking fun at other people, showing them up; but in the long run it turns sour. On the other hand, we never will get tired of listening to you tell stories on yourself.

Geraldine Taylor wrote about her father-in-law, Hudson Taylor, as if he were a plaster saint. When John Pollock did some research in Taylor's life, he found that Geraldine Taylor had deliberately left out material she thought might "offend the weak Christian." So Hudson Taylor came off as a super-saint, if not a spook. But in his letters, Pollock found Taylor to be very human indeed, and he brought out some of the man's humor.

The 20th century will not put up with phony imagery. You can write as a proud Christian and try to impress readers, but they will see through it. There is no joy in conning people into thinking you are better than you are. "God opposes the proud but gives grace to the humble" (James 4:6).

Go for the humor. We will reach the sinner with a chuckle a lot quicker than with a whiff of sulphur. Even more than humor, let's try to convey in our writing something of the serene joy we have that we are on our way to heaven. Neither tragedies nor the gold medals of this life are the final measurement. We are excited about the great things in store for those who know and love and obey the Lord Jesus Christ. I know they will tell us we are crazy, but a hundred years from now we will be checking our books out of the library of heaven and saying, "Who's crazy now?"

3

BEGINNING TO THINK PROFESSIONALLY

Something exciting happened recently in New Zealand. For the first time in the nation's history a Christian Writers' Guild was formed, and a School of Writing held that drew from all over the two islands. One of the principal speakers at that school was John Kennedy, editor of the Catholic *Tablet* and one of the prominent citizens of the country. I was privileged to be part of the faculty, and after the closing luncheon I expressed to Mr. Kennedy my appreciation for his contribution and remarked, "Here we are from different traditions working together in a common Christian effort."

His reply was, "It's all done on a professional level."

I have since reflected on the words of my colleague and have studied to learn what it means to be a professional in the writing field. Does it mean that the beliefs we hold dear suddenly don't matter? Surely not! Well, then, is there really a plane upon which we can function that is different from our individual spiritual allegiances and also from the personal obstacles that hold us back as writers? Is there a different level based on skill and competence where not only our particular theological convictions but our timidities, our feelings of inadequacy, our prejudices, our jealousies and resentments, our specialized quirks and idiosyncrasies can be left behind, without in the least compromising our faith, for the sake of getting the work done that God has given us to do?

I believe there is. It may not be suitable always in the pulpit, where particular loyalties must be acknowledged, but it's available to us as writers. And I believe that if we can attain that professional level, it will help us enormously in our struggle with the written word.

In reading the Gospels it is useful to note the way our Lord dealt with professional people, with soldiers and tax collectors and fishermen. Professional people have always been different, the difference being their total absorption in their work. And I've noticed that when a Christian who seeks to become a published writer begins to think professionally, much of the frustration and disappointment connected with the writing business evaporates.

Writing for publication is a mysterious business with plenty of traps and pitfalls, and we who are engaged in it are particularly susceptible to disappointment. We may go home from Christian writers' conferences muttering, "A thousand shall sell at my side, and ten thousand at my right hand, but I'll never make it." We all know that negative feelings can weaken incentive, but when one blow comes after another, that old sinking feeling takes over. That's why I would like you now quietly to resolve to think of yourself henceforward as a free-lance professional writer. Repeat it after me: *"I am a free-lance professional writer!"*

What do we mean by the word *professional*? How does the pro differ from the amateur? Is it the money one takes in? The fact that one is using a word processor? That one is a cousin of some publisher? No. It takes more than a snorkel to make a skin diver, and I am not now thinking about the kind of equipment a writer works with or how many contracts one has signed. A track record is important; tools are important; a buyer and an editor are important. The craftsman needs these things; but even more important is the interior attitude the writer takes in approaching the craft and settling in to do a job of work.

The ancient Greek aristocrats ran a slave society and took a contemptuous view of work. They sat around on Mars Hill in their togas and made fun of the artisans who built the Parthenon. Today in America we hold the leisure class of aristocrats in contempt. We call them parasites. We ask, what do they do?

But when we see real pros at work, we admire them tremendously. I once watched Joe DiMaggio of the New York Yankees in action and came away amazed at his competence and professional skill. It's a homey feeling, this being a pro—not a proud feeling, but neither is it a nervous, anxious, or wistful feeling. It's a comfortable feeling that bespeaks confidence in one's knowledgeability and expertise. The Old Testament prophets called it wisdom. I think that is why we like to watch Jesus Christ as he appears in the Gospels: he was such a pro in the business of living.

How does the pro differ from the amateur? Let me reminisce a moment. At the age of 24 I was earning $15 a week (plus carfare) as a reporter for William Randolph Hearst on the San Francisco *Examiner*. I was not a Christian. In desperation I decided to take the future in my hands and strike out for Alaska. So I typed letters to 50 or 60 magazines around the country, telling them who I was and offering to send them stories about Alaska. A very few answered my letter and advised me to stay home. Only one editor showed interest. He published the Wisconsin *Dairyman* and thought he'd like to know more about the cows in Matanuska Valley.

I was disappointed, but went anyway. I took a bus to Seattle and bought a steerage ticket to Juneau, where my money ran out. On arrival in port I put on a clean shirt, walked down to the local newspaper office, and talked my way into a job as city editor. Writing those letters was an amateurish approach. Talking my way into a job was acting professionally.

So thinking and acting professionally means, I would say, first of all going for the personal contact. It's well known that Americans like to do business on a first-name basis. Millionaires prefer not to make their big deals in the office. They make them at lunch or on the golf course or in a private plane—some place where they can't be overheard or bugged. Another well-known fact is that many important people don't answer their mail. At Christian writing schools you will be told how to write a query letter, and that is important. However, you will get faster action if you have coffee with the editor.

That's my way of saying that magazines and publishing houses receive a lot of mail from people like you. They know if they answer it, it's going to mean a lot more mail; so if they can, they unload it on someone else down the line. If you catch the editor in a social situation—meet her at a conference, take him to lunch, sit next to her on an airplane, get to know him socially—and he learns something of your ideas and spirit and eventually your writing style, you might just strike fire.

Are you timid about this? Does it require more boldness than you have to approach an editor and say, "Could I have a moment of your time?" Maybe you need to feel desperate—desperate enough to buy a steerage ticket to Alaska. Thinking professionally doesn't always mean typing up an impressive two-page, single-spaced resumé and mailing it along with a self-addressed envelope with a commemorative stamp. It means being brazen enough to make a contact.

Do you recall the story Jesus told in Luke 18 about a city widow who had a problem? She felt someone was trying to rip her off, and decided to do something about it. So what did she do? Dial a prayer? Hire a lawyer? File a complaint with the city council? Sue the realty board? Call the sheriff? Write the newspaper? Spill it all on a talk-in show? Go on "Sixty Minutes"? Talk to a minister? No. She wrapped a shawl around her head and went straight to the judge. Now, the judge fought her off. He couldn't stand her, she was bad news in 48-point type. But she laid it on him and got what she wanted. She was a real pro.

Thinking professionally also means not being afraid to ask for help from other people. There are no ivory towers for Christian writers. You'll never make it in an attic garret. We writers have to make ourselves vulnerable and mix with people—all kinds of people—or our writing will not be as good as it ought to be. Thinking professionally then means laying oneself open, asking questions, following leads, digging out information, leaning on sources, not depending solely on oneself.

Critique groups can help a lot here. I have sat in scores of critique groups, and I have never yet read something to a group without receiving suggestions that improved what I was working on. It's not a matter of finding a congenial group or mixing with so-called advanced writers; it's a matter of being willing to listen and receive help. I will have more to say on this subject in Chapter 16. If you are one of those people who is sure you know what you want to say and how you want to say it, if you prefer not to be under obligation to anyone, if you don't need any help, then I'm afraid this point misses you. But the pros that I know got that way by learning from others. The Bible says that God resists the proud but gives grace to the humble.

The editor of the Miami *Herald* was vice-chairperson of the Billy Graham Crusade when he lived in San Diego. He told some of us that recently he went to Peru and was put up in a luxury hotel. He had never been to the country and wanted to see something of it, so he hired a cab to take him to one of the crowded *barrios* that cluster around Lima, where millions of poor people live. The first driver refused to take him and his friend, but eventually they got there and made contact with a ragged priest. He asked the priest, "What can you do for these people?"

"Nothing!" replied the priest.

But my friend is a pro, and he got his story. He went back home and wrote it. As a result, without his solicitation, enough money was contributed by readers of his paper to support that priest for three years.

Thinking professionally will not only make us bold to seek contacts and make us humble to seek help from other people; it also gives us a handle on adversity—and believe me, that comes to all of us. Every pro has dry spells and slumps. We writers experience rejection slips, sometimes three in one day. But the real pro doesn't wait for something good to come in the mail. The real pro puts adversity to work.

First of all, pros take the rejection philosophically, knowing that battle scars have to be expected in this business. I knew a lawyer of whom it was said he never lost a case—because he never tried one. The only writers who never get rejections are those who never send out anything. But true professionals will simply not let the hurt get to them, any more than a shortstop who bobbles a grounder will sit down and weep. We wrap ourselves in an invisible shield of our own self-knowledge. We can write; we have the skill. There's just something lacking, and if we can find it, we have the qualifications to make our writing work.

In 1984 I sat in the Los Angeles Coliseum during the tryouts for the American Olympic team. One of the pole vaulters missed twice at 17'10". One more miss and he was through, this 19-foot vaulter. He tried once more and cleared it. The man sitting next to us happened to be a track coach who had a vaulter in the competition. I said to him after that third leap, "You know, I didn't think he was going to make it. He didn't seem to have enough power in his lift as he went up."

The man told me, "He didn't. He went over on his technique."

A real pro doesn't have to try harder, but has to work on technique, that's all. And so we take criticism objectively, and thank God when it's constructive. Most editors prefer not to involve themselves in explaining their reasons for rejecting a writer, lest they be drawn into argument. But I can assure you that if editors do not feel threatened, and if they are approached in the right way, they will gladly share their thoughts with you. Editors are not ogres; they really want to help writers because they like us; and furthermore, if it weren't for us they would have nothing to publish!

One publishing house sent me a contract and advance for a book, and I spent two years writing it. When I finally submitted it, they rejected it, canceled the contract, but told me I could keep the advance. They sent me a two-page letter explaining what was wrong with the manuscript and quoting outside reviewers. I spent that night—well, you can imagine how I spent it. But next day I telephoned New York and asked if I could try again. I told them their criticisms had merit. They said I could try again, and they would leave the contract in force. It took seven months to rewrite the manuscript, but when it was finally published, *Eternity* magazine made it their book of the year. That would never have happened if it had been published in its original form. Make adversity work for you!

Professional writers also protect their interests by the way they conduct their business affairs. They behave honorably and expect their editors and publishers to do the same. They do not build grudges or run down a particular house, or play off one publisher against another. The pro is like a caribou that comes to a waterhole and finds it dry. It doesn't get mad, it just looks for another waterhole. You send your manuscript to an editor who has asked for it, and then after a while you learn that the editor has left and the new editor doesn't know anything about it and can't find it. That happens all the time. Or the publisher accepts your book and then goes out of business. When these things occur, pros don't lose their cool, they just extricate themselves and look elsewhere. When a pitcher gets mad at the umpire, you know what happens to his pitching. The professional also avoids the traps that get amateurs in trouble—plagiarism, quoting without permission, upsetting other members of a subject's family, libelous statements, failing to show one's subject what will come out in print. Even when one changes the name of a subject, it's good to have permission in writing. And, of course, the copyright laws must be observed and credit lines given. All this becomes second nature, the detail that a writer takes in stride.

Professional writers concentrate on the reader audience. I visit a lot of critique groups still, and I find the amateurs present have one common characteristic: they are engrossed in themselves and not in their readership. Is my writing good? Do you like it? Do I get my point across? Do you think I have talent? That's what they want to know, and none of it matters. The real question is, is there a demand for it? Where could I send it? Is it salable? If not, why not? Where are the flaws in it? Where are the strengths? Have I slanted it toward the market I have in mind? Have I kept myself out of it except where I naturally fit in? Have I made my subject human, or have I drawn him or her as a holy specter? Is this topic still interesting to people? The professional always has one eye on the copy and the other on the market.

There are at least 10 million would-be writers in our country, and their standard procedure with a book is to turn out 100 or 200 or 500 pages and then ask, "Where shall I send it?" I followed that procedure for 25 years and was rewarded by nothing but disappointment. But the professional will take the advice of my friend Norman Rohrer who says, "Sell it, then write it."

Finally, professionals give every piece they write their best shot. There is a valid professional pride and it is good. True pros take satisfaction in a successful performance and are unhappy with a mediocre one. Whatever their field of endeavor, they seek to honor their craft. The goal is not perfection; the world contains very few masterpieces in literature or anything else. But let's not mail anything to an editor that doesn't represent our best effort at the time. That may require a lot of rewriting, especially if the editor sends it back.

Since retiring, I wrote a piece for *Decision* magazine, which I edited for 16 years, and it came back with a rejection. Instead of grinding my teeth, I read it over and decided it could be even funnier. So I retyped it, and another magazine took it, and it has been reprinted several times. And that's not a bad approach to your next reject: do it over and make it more entertaining!

Let me remind you in closing of Jesus Christ. While he was constantly teaching his disciples how to love each other, he showed them how to do it with class, with skill—putting up the wounded man at the inn, washing people's feet, praising the use of ointment, killing the fatted calf, and in so many ways showing them the way not just to love properly, or civilly, or even benevolently, but rather with expertise, with a flourish—with a professional touch. May our writing in its final form be such that when one day it is presented to Christ, it will receive his, "Well done, good and faithful servant. You're a real pro!"

4

THE WORLD OF A WRITER

At the beginning I suggested that Christianity has inspired the most beautiful music ever heard by human ears, the finest in architecture and art, the sublimest passions, and the noblest spirit of sacrifice in people, and I asked, Why shouldn't it evoke great writing?

I believe God is telling us to take the wraps off the gospel. He is calling his writers to fill the gap and move in. He is saying in effect, "This is your hour in the world. The media are yours. If your copy measures up, it will be read by kings and governors. To you I am giving an unprecedented opportunity to sow the seed of the gospel so it will multiply around the globe."

Why don't we pick up the challenge? It will mean ceasing our nitpicking at other Christians. It will put an end to editorials about rising postal rates. God wants us to let our ribbons scorch the paper as we tell the world what he has done, is doing now, and will do—according to his Word.

The time is ripe for moving into positions of spiritual, intellectual, and cultural leadership in the world, where we become chaplains to the reading public. No one else is in the field except the horoscope writers. So in addition to shipping young, God-fearing missionaries up the Orinoco, let's catapult them into the mass media.

Young Christians should be infiltrating the field of communications, taking over posts of leadership, moving up and moving in—not by craftiness but by craft; not by supernatural intervention so much as by the fact that they are the best in the business.

Most evangelicals today are writing for other evangelicals. That is a needy market, but fresh ground is waiting to be broken. Somebody also needs to speak with the authentic voice of the gospel of Jesus Christ to a world of culture.

C. S. Lewis made a breakthrough, and today his influence is greater than at the time of his death in 1963. God is looking for a younger Lewis who has a willingness to master written expression, someone who (to rewrite Kipling) can walk with commoners, nor lose the kingly touch; someone who can do with arts and letters what Billy Graham does with the spoken word—shock the world with truth.

Henry Zylstra once asked, "How can we create a Christian literature without so limiting it as to make it trivial and unimportant?" There in capsule is the whole problem.

If I were to escort a well-read, non-Christian friend into one of our typical Bible bookstores, I would blush. Not that the store is unattractive; far from it. But what could I show him? Whose work would challenge him? I am speaking now not of the simplicity Jesus honored, but of the simpleness we get by with, the trivia our publishers sell because they cannot get anything better from us.

If we are to communicate to the late 20th century, we will have to do better. Two types of persons exemplify the goals we seek. The first is the Renaissance individual. In seeking the qualities that the media most admire and wish to emulate, I keep coming back to the Renaissance.

People with this background do not have encyclopedic knowledge so much as encyclopedic interest. They are the connoisseurs, even the dilettantes. They are the William Buckley type, who seems comfortably at home in any field of human inquiry, or the George Plimpton type, who is game for anything.

These individuals are persons of wide-ranging interest, of polish, of sophistication, of manners, of taste, of humor. They make strong points in a gentle, telling manner. They are civilized; they don't "lose their cool." They know history, languages, poets, scientists, sports. They are the beautiful people, cultured, cultivated, educated, charming.

Contrasting are the people of Reformation background. These people originated in the same period of history but are different. They are persons of God's Book, of unrelenting purpose and moral passion, with the gleam of eternity in their eyes. Reformation people are not those of pleasantries, but those of action. They are God's prophets. They proclaim the gospel of Jesus Christ, the glad tidings of great joy.

Reformation people also pierce our consciences, warn us of hell and judgment, and bid us repent and be saved. To them the media are tools provided by God, to be used by his Spirit while there is time before the end to draw men, women, and children into the kingdom.

My feeling is that Christian writers of the late 20th century should seek to combine the Renaissance and the Reformation. We cannot do without the one or the other. The Renaissance person identifies with the readers but may have nothing to proclaim to them; the Reformation person has the proclamation but so often cannot identify with the people he or she wishes to reach.

Why do we need to be Renaissance people? Because the Western world has fallen into a cultural and spiritual morass. One does not need to read Capote or Nabokov or Updike to discover that. In journalism the gap that is yawning between the American news media and the public is more than a disparity between leftist intellectualism and middle-class conservatism. We are just not being well informed!

Some of the journalists, editors, newscasters, and commentators who serve us are cultural nincompoops. They seem to have little sense of history. They do not know their Toynbee. Apparently they are ignorant of the classics. They seldom quote the Bible. They are practicing monolinguists; they rarely refer to any other culture.

If they travel, it seems to be from one Hilton bar to another. When they are required to take an editorial stand, they can locate no point of reference, and so they mount their chargers and ride off in all directions.

I say the Christian writers engaged in journalism should be Renaissance persons who know more about culture and history and custom than the skeptical reporters alongside them. They should know the English language and the writers who have mastered it. Journalism courses are no substitute for a grasp of American and European literature.

The Christian writer should know more about this world than the worldly writer, even though the Christian does not belong to this world and is looking for a better one. The Christian writer should know, for example, what has made the American system of government work and a hundred others fall. That means an acquaintance with Montesquieu's *Spirit of the Laws*, as well as with the doctrine of original sin as James Madison learned it in the classroom of the Reverend John Witherspoon at the College of New Jersey.

How much culture? It is impossible to say; one's education is never completed. I am not suggesting an unattainable reading program. But surely the writer is impoverished who has never dipped into Chaucer, Shakespeare, Milton, Pascal, Swift, Johnson, or Browning, to name just a handful. Malcolm Muggeridge has told us how much he owes to certain Christian writers: to Augustine, Bunyan, Kierkegaard, Weil, Bonhoeffer, and others.

Now let us look again at the Reformation type—God's man or God's woman in today's world. More than anything else, the communications industry needs Christian writers who are committed to what John A. Mackay calls "the majesty of truth." Their concept of truth would be formed by him who said, "I am the truth." Their function would be not only to sort out fact from opinion but to distinguish fact from rumor, fact from gossip, fact from character assassination. They would be committed to the proposition that truth exists, and that truth is in relation to goodness.

The Reformation writer turned journalist should be the most accurate and dependable person in the business. It was said of the great baseball pitcher Christy Mathewson that if he was in a game and the umpires had a close decision to make, they would ask his opinion, even though he was a competitor, because he had such a reputation for honesty. That should be the Reformation person—eager to find the facts, determined to be fair, quick to acknowledge errors, and zealous of the truth.

The Reformation writer should not take advantage of his assignment to preach doctrine if he is not invited to preach, but that does not mean he cannot honor the Bible, or express Christian convictions about the issues of our day, or help as well as inform, or in some basic way try to lift the burdens of the people by pointing to the sources of relief. God help him if he doesn't!

I would expect the Reformation person to assume in every story he writes that right is better than wrong, faith is better than doubt, courage is better than fear, joy is better than grief, and love is better than hate. I would expect him to circulate encouraging news wherever he finds it and to avoid sensational and inflammatory treatment of news that is not in the public interest.

An urgent need in religious publications is to go back to the Bible and start preaching salvation by grace. Many who are reading Christian literature need strong meat, and we keep on feeding them pablum.

Some of the religious publications in North America are in trouble because they have stopped being themselves. They are no longer interpreting life spiritually but have become like everyone else. When people pick up a religious paper, they expect it to say something about God. They expect it to approach the problems of life from a spiritual standpoint. The decks may be awash and the ship sinking, but they expect Christian writers to be manning the lifeboats for Jesus.

Many of these readers are unconsciously looking for help. When they find religious papers reflecting what they read everywhere else, they lay them down.

Finally, we are at our creative best when we are in communication with others who spark our imaginations and give wings to our ideas. The picture of the lonely genius in his pad, scribbling away at deathless prose, is not quite accurate. Even though writing is best done in solitude, it remains a social activity. Out of the milieu of common activity emerges the genius. Shakespeare would be unthinkable without the Age of Elizabeth, and Bunyan without the Reformation. So it is important that the Christian writer become like the caliph of Baghdad, Haroun al-Raschid, who slipped out of his castle in disguise to find out what people were saying and doing.

Paul moved easily in the atmosphere of his times, reading the literature, following the Olympic Games. So must we. Yet it will not be easy, for the surroundings are polluted, and Christians are to keep themselves unspotted from the world.

It could be pointed out that Shakespeare, Goethe, Tolstoy, Dostoevsky, Wordsworth, Solzhenitsyn, and C. S. Lewis are not considered "evangelicals" in the usual sense of the term. But these are writers equipped with a range of imagination, with fertile powers that are not necessarily conferred on persons by virtue of their faith. If we reject these writers, we reject a genuine source of artistic, mental, and theological inspiration. We make it harder to do really creative Christian writing because we pass up an important point of contact with the world we are seeking to reach for Jesus Christ.

It is no easy task, this wrestling with an alien culture that is saturated with the principle of evil. Sometimes we are sorely tempted to withdraw and spend our time writing private devotional thoughts. But even then, the best devotions come not from the cloister but (as with Brother Lawrence) from the kitchen.

Remember this: God did commit to us the saving message of the gospel. We are not religious hacks trying to milk the public with a special brand of esoteric teaching. We may be vessels of mud, but we are commissioned to carry the divine treasure. That commission is what makes us servants of truth and stewards of the mysteries of grace. At the very least it ought to make us readable writers.

5

FOUR KEYS TO SUCCESSFUL WRITING

So far we have been thinking about attitudes: How should the writer look at himself and what approach should he take to his material? How should he understand his frame of reference—the cultural situation in which he finds himself? Now we are ready for action. The sweatsuits come off; we are about to enter the race.

In this chapter I will set forth four keys which, if the writer grasps them and uses them, will make the writer a successful, published author. You may not have a polished education; you may not have a high intelligence quotient, you may not have "talent" (whatever that is), you may be poor, and live far from the marts of trade, but I guarantee that you will publish and that people will read what you write.

Motivation: The First Key

Why should a person write? Why should we bother to spend interminable hours wriggling fingers at a typewriter or word processor, inserting sheets and filling wastebaskets? What are we trying to prove? And who in heaven or on earth cares? It's one thing to have an assignment, a deadline, an eager editor stroking us with lovely words of expectation and encouragement, but many writers have to hack it without such amenities. While groping along the twisting corridors of our thinking, we manage to stumble on an idea and assume that it is not only worthy, it is original, unique, and altogether magnificent. It must be "written up," whether we get encouragement or not.

It's hard to say what our motive is. Let's leave for the moment our lofty goals, our personal spiritual commitment, and our far-ranging life purposes. Let's make it clear that we're not in it simply for fame or money. C. S. Lewis told me that writing is a lust; it is "scratching where you itch." Perhaps he got that from Robert Browning's "Epistle of Karshish, the Arab Physician":

> I half resolve to tell thee, yet I blush,
> What set me off a-writing first of all.
> An itch I had, a sting to write, a tang!

And I guess many of us would confess that we write simply because we have to. We're "word people," and if we cannot preach like Peter or pray like Paul, at least we can write like the devil. But the devil doesn't have us; we are on the battlefield for our Lord. How, then, do we justify our calling as writers?

We begin by returning to our personal spiritual commitment. Christian writers believe that Jesus Christ, who gives meaning to everything in life, gives meaning and purpose to their writing. From him we receive the Spirit of the Lord. What then is our motive? Our motive is to spread the blessings of the Christian message. Rather than proclaim the gospel from the housetops, which seems a singularly ineffective medium in our day, we prefer the printed page. We believe that in the teachings of Jesus Christ, and even more in his life, death, and resurrection, our Creator was unfolding to the human race the mystery of our existence and the key to our survival.

So we are bearers in the nuclear age of a life-and-death message. No matter what the literary form, the message remains the same: Jesus Christ died to save sinners. And while the message is being channeled through many media, we remain committed to the written word, because we are convinced of its power. Many major changes in the recorded history of the planet have been brought about through literature. Let me mention a few writings that have shaped human destiny: the Ten Commandments, the *Analects* of Confucius, the New Testament, the Koran, the *Imitation of Christ*, *Pilgrim's Progress*, the Declaration of Independence, *Uncle Tom's Cabin*, *The Origin of Species*, the *Communist Manifesto*, *Mein Kampf*. To these could be added any number of less significant writings that have influenced their time.

The very existence of the Christian church is dependent on the writings that were first penned, then preserved in a way that no others have been kept. In an age when so much emphasis is being placed on evangelism by radio and TV, we need to remind ourselves of the permanence of the printed page. In any local library you can communicate with the great thinkers of history whose words have come down to us. A hundred years from now Billy Graham may be remembered not by his films, crusades, videotapes, newspaper columns, or tracts, but by his books. They'll be there till Jesus comes.

What a challenge to us to join that noble caravan and transmit to posterity our own legacy of thought! What a thrill to think that something we write might influence a life or even save a generation! I was fascinated to find in Montesquieu's *Spirit of the Laws* the precise formula for the division of powers (legislative, executive, judicial) that was adopted by the framers of our American Constitution. This Frenchman, writing quietly at his home near Bordeaux in the 1740s, actually designed the American republic! Our founding fathers simply copied his ideas.

Our motive, then, is to produce Christian writing that is action literature, not only inspiring but also efficacious. We want to see things happen, to watch the Spirit of God sway opinion and change people's lives by turning them around. We want to warn, to inform, to encourage, by precept and admonition and parable and poem and every known literary device. It's true we are enthusiasts. The Marxists invade the literary forms to propagandize for their own ends; we do so for the kingdom of God.

We want things to happen, because we care. We want to help. We are concerned about other people, living out their lives in "quiet desperation." What we lack in genius we make up for in earnestness of purpose. Do not classify us as reformers so much as healers and teachers, following Jesus of Nazareth. We find it hard to "live and let live" when we encounter every day so much trouble and suffering. Other writers, not necessarily religious, are also concerned with human need. We don't presume to preempt the field; we simply wish to make clear our motive: to take hold of one small corner of the human burden and lift, together with anyone else who will join us.

Part of our motive is wrapped up in the poor quality of much current reading material. Words can save, but words can also corrupt. The pornography market is mushrooming and has reached the status of a multi-billion-dollar industry; in the United States alone it is estimated that 90 million copies of porn literature are published and circulated every month. It has invaded all the major bookstores. What used to be passed furtively from hand to hand is now advertised and reviewed in the most respectable publications. Christian bookstore owners tell of people coming into their stores and asking, "In God's name, have you anything decent to read?"

We Christian writers find ourselves swimming not against a current but against a massive flood. We look for words of principle such as *virtue, modesty, honor, reverence,* and even *integrity,* only to find they have been made a laughingstock and torn to shreds. But we don't care. Our lives are not our own. We have been claimed by the Holy Spirit, and given the same orders he gave to Habakkuk: "Write down the revelation and make it plain" (Hab. 2:2).

So writing becomes an important part of our ministry. We are commissioned not just to write evil down, but to write God up. We are instructed to teach, to train, to interpret, to inform, to edify, to kindle the imagination, to narrate stories as Jesus did, and even to entertain. We are to provide milk for children, solid food for full-grown men and women, and the nectar of poetry to express our love for our Creator. We are to write about frustration and victory, justice and mercy, sin and redemption, joy and adversity, and always grace and glory. We are to give people a handle to grasp as they seek to attain a worthwhile and productive existence under Christ.

Out there in the reading public, you will find, are millions of people who are looking for something to read that will make them better than they are. They want something that will uplift them, give them a new hope, a fresh horizon, a glimpse of what they were made for. They are waiting for us. If we can meet their demand for quality, we will be bought and read.

So we draw our motivation not only from divine mandate but also from human yearning. A taste gap exists in much of the literature that is being produced today. We Christian writers wish we were better qualified to fill it, but fill it we shall, because as long as there is language, there will be readers. Many of these people will never come to church; they will never be touched by preaching or music, by radio or television or cassettes. They are waiting for us to write the word and make it plain, that they may read and know the truth.

Contacts: The Second Key

As you are drawn deeper into the writing game, you will learn that the writer lives by encouragement. Writing is essentially a lonely profession, and when the rejections pile up and the interest flags, the writer slides easily into the blues. To all such writers I have one suggestion: cover your machine, walk out the door, and go calling. Either that, or pick up the telephone. If possible, talk to an editor or another writer.

I have often said that getting into print is like getting into heaven: it's not what we do but whom we know. In today's world most business is carried on by personal contact. Someone knows someone. To be in touch with the right person at the right time with the right ability and skill to meet a need is to be a success in the writing field, as in many another profession.

Thousands, even millions, of aspiring writers are eating their hearts out because they spent hundreds of hours on a manuscript and can't find anyone to publish it. I know that route all too well, and I can tell you it is a dead end. The worst mistake you might make as a writer is to hole up in a cabin for a period of time and write a book. Every week people come to me and say, "I've written a book, now what do I do? I've sent it here and there and it comes back." I shake my head, and sometimes I say, "Let's put that manuscript on the shelf and just talk about your idea."

Or I might say, "Have you visited the editor of your local paper? He may not be a Christian, but you should get acquainted with him." Believe me, that is an exciting prospect. I can tell you many stories of Christian writers who have taken that tip and are now writing columns once or twice a week, and being paid for them. It took time to cultivate the editor, but eventually it paid off.

Go to a writers' conference and meet the editors. Visit them in their offices and take them to lunch. Get on a first-name basis with them, if it seems appropriate. Then broach your article idea, or your book idea, and if they don't shoot it down in flames, they may publish it. That's the way it's done—through friendship. Sending a query letter to an editor is good, but getting to know one and sounding out him or her is better. When it comes to being accepted for publication, so often the contact is the key.

You will find that editors are not impersonal people who delight in sending rejection notices. They like writers and want to help them. They don't like being inundated with unsolicited manuscripts, but they are always looking for fresh ideas.

It's amazing what an editor's interest will do for a writer. It is rare that an editor will buy a manuscript before seeing it completed, but he or she will often give the writer hope. The editor will read early chapters and lend advice, and will encourage the writer to submit work "on speculation." That does wonders for the writer's morale. No longer is he groping in the dark, trying to break into print as an unknown, facing a hostile market.

I am not suggesting that because you live next door to an editor, that guarantees your access to authorship, but it certainly doesn't hurt! Meanwhile, you can make friends with people you meet in writers' groups and attend editors' workshops and visit the publisher of your national church paper or magazine—not to try to unload your writing, but to learn what people in the publishing world are looking for, and then try in a modest way to meet some of their needs.

Once you have broken the ice, once your article or story or poem has been accepted, then it is vitally important to follow up. Keep the editorial contact warm! Use letters, use the telephone, use visits. Make it clear you are willing and available, in case the editor has an assignment. Your writing career is cumulative; the more you appear in print, the more you will be used. You may not be writing the thing you want to write, but that can wait. After you are established and you have given the editor what is required, you will have earned the right to suggest a topic close to your heart, and the editor will listen.

Discipline: The Third Key

Discipline is the natural outflow of motivation. What we want badly enough, we are usually willing to work for. The difficulty is that we want so many things, and our schedule becomes crowded. I can tell you, for example, that all of the great preachers of the past hundred years made their reputations not through their pulpit oratory but through their writing. It is quite true. Not even television has changed this fact. I can tell you that every great movement in the history of the world that has brought change has been accomplished through writing—at least since the alphabet came into use. Yet all this will not sway you and cause you to become a writer—not if you tell me there simply isn't time!

That is where discipline comes in. If, for example, you swing into the habit of writing something every day, your literary output will increase markedly. Some authors rise early to write; others prefer the evening. Dostoevsky's custom was to write all night, beginning at midnight. The hour is not important; the discipline is. The temptations that beset a writer are infinite. A free-lance writer I know says that when he is composing on the typewriter, he often paces about the house and usually finds himself meditating either in front of the refrigerator or in the bed. But books are not written in beds or around iceboxes.

Discipline is especially vital in establishing the accuracy of what you write. To get up from your chair and check a source or a fact is not easy, but it is better than relying on memory. Shortcuts in research mean that we are relying on guesswork, and writers cannot get away with that. Your writing research will make you a better communicator. It will also make you respected for the truth of your writing.

The most important application of discipline to the writing profession is in rewriting. You may recall that when King Jehoiakim of Israel burned the scroll that contained the words of the prophet Jeremiah, the prophet dictated another scroll that contained all the words that had been destroyed, *and added many similar words*, according to the record (Jer. 36:32). In other words, the second draft was an improvement on the first. To go over what you have written inevitably means to make it better. Very few writers can turn out clean copy at the first writing. To rewrite is the first law of the profession.

The word processor has made it easy to insert corrections in one's copy, but it has not noticeably improved the general quality of writing. To begin again, to start from scratch, to use the first typing simply as a basis for a thorough revision, is to guarantee a superior product. We are just not that good the first time around. If we have a tight deadline with no time to polish, we must crank out the copy and let it go. That may bring some quick cash, but it will not produce literature. Good writing calls for discipline. Sentences need to be changed. Adjectives need to be taken out. More precise language, or more exciting language, needs to be substituted. You can do all kinds of things on the rewrite to make your copy better, but it means work.

Suppose you have an idea, and jot it down on the back of an envelope. You take the idea to your machine and bang it out in a few paragraphs. That is only the first step. Leave it overnight and the next day, use a fresh sheet and rephrase it, expanding as you go. Do that three or four times, and you might have something fit to read to someone else. Then after it has been critiqued, go over it again. Now your discipline is beginning to pay off. You have found a key to eventual success.

Tools: The Fourth Key

No professional can do his best work without sharp tools. A scalpel with a razor edge, clean lumber, quality paints, a well-oiled machine can make all the difference.

It's true that some authors have turned out masterpieces in prison; others have written in rooms filled with relatives and crying babies; millions of manuscripts have been turned out in longhand. I admire all such, but have no desire to imitate. My output comes hard enough without making it more difficult. At some pains I have personally collected what I consider the proper tools and equipment for a Christian writer to turn out salable work. When I come into my study and sit down to work, it is a pleasurable experience.

Tools will not, of course, substitute for ideas. Tools will not inspire. C. S. Lewis wrote better with a nib pen than I ever will with the latest Xerox Memorywriter. But I can do better on my machine than I could with a nib pen, and I feel much more like doing it. The craftsman equips himself for his craft.

Motivation alone, contacts alone, discipline alone, and tools alone will not make the successful writer, but *together they will;* I guarantee it. Of course we must then ask, what is success? For the Christian the quintessential element in writing is the message itself—its content, its significance. The Creator has given his children the gift of language and has told us to use it to spread the truth of his salvation. The same God gave us the Bible in written form, and kept it through the centuries that we might use it to rescue a lost humanity from its own self-destruction. Now, if God used writing, why shouldn't we?

People come to our churches, they hear our sermons, and often they leave unmoved. But on their way out the door they may pick up a tract, a testimony, or a book, and read it quietly in solitude. As they read, the Spirit of God speaks to them. They may return to church with a fresh outlook, perhaps even a new heart. It happens all the time. Kenneth Strachan, the late founder of Evangelism in Depth, told me that nine out of ten Latin Americans come to Christ through the reading of some form of Christian literature.

A popular Anglican divine of the 17th century, Thomas Fuller, related a story about a "devout but ignorant" Christian who lived in Spain and faithfully said each day his Paternoster and Ave Maria. The man knew he was also supposed to add his own prayers to God, but he didn't know how. Instead, each morning he would get on his knees and lift his eyes and hands to heaven and solemnly repeat the alphabet! Then he would say, "Now, O good God, put these letters together to spell syllables and words that make such sense as may be most to your glory and my good."

May the Lord in his mercy do as much for all of us.

6

WHAT THE READERS WANT

I believe that if there are enough good writers and good publishing houses, people will buy books and read them. I believe that good Christian literature is always acceptable, outside the church as well as inside. Today the public is more receptive than ever to our writing.

Editors are looking for people who are aware of the times in which they live, and who are not writing the way their mothers wrote, who are not turning out eighth-grade compositions, but who are writing in the modern vein. The editors want material that is alive, that pulses with a feeling that you know where you are—not in some ivory tower, but right downtown on the mall. They want Christ in the marketplace.

The editors also want material that appeals to young people. But some writers don't realize this, so they write for the dear folks at home, sitting in their swing in the garden, rocking back and forth and reading pleasant little devotionals. We need, instead, a youthful, zestful frame of mind.

The editors want copy also that has a fresh approach. A young man came to one of our writing schools, an athletic type, and I said to him, "Why don't you collect testimonies from famous athletes in America and publish them as a daily devotional?" A Christian house picked up the idea and published it. Now he has finished his second book and is working on his third.

How can we put our copy into marketable shape? How does the writer get his vehicle off the launching pad and his writing into orbit? I would list three stages for this rocket.

The first is, *make contact with the reader.* If we are going to make contact with today's reader, we cannot hide ourselves, as our Victorian ancestors did, behind the discreet hedge of pious expressions, asides to the gentle reader, and all that sort of thing. There are no more gentle readers; they are all watching television. If people take the trouble to scan what you have written, do you know what they are going to be looking for? I know modern readers. They will wonder, "Why is this person writing this thing? What's he or she up to?" Many readers don't think that we really care about them. They want to know, "What's this person's angle?" Make contact, and make a positive contact.

More than 40 years ago I signed on as a quartermaster aboard an 80-feet Bureau of Fisheries vessel in the Gulf of Alaska. It was a convenient way for me to get from Valdez to Juneau across the Gulf of Alaska, a two-day trip, but it turned out to be the worst voyage of my life. We ran into a howling storm; it took us a week to get there. When I got to the end of that journey, I wrote the story and sent it to the *Alaska Sportsman,* a magazine published in Ketchikan, Alaska. The editor fired it back to me with this comment: "So you had a miserable time. Why inflict it on others?" Be careful that you don't take advantage of your facile pen to get rid of what is bothering you. Don't take your miseries and parade them in front of other people, trying to attract sympathy (that is what I was trying to do, so that the natural interest of the storm and the voyage was lost in the shower of tears).

The next stage is the *organizing of material.*

Three books in my filing cabinet never got off the launching pad. One was written during my years in Alaska. It has a light, easy narrative style; it has adventure; it has color; it makes contact with the reader. It was sent to many different publishers, and it bounced back. Finally, I arranged for a woman who had worked for Macmillan to read it for a ten-dollar fee. She told me, "This manuscript is not organized." I knew it, but I did not know what to do about it, and anyway I felt that stylistically it was such a gem that it did not really matter.

"Young man," said H. G. Wells to an aspiring young writer, "you have a style before you have a story, and God help you." I had the last interview with C. S. Lewis before he died. I asked him, "Will you tell young writers something about style?" He said, "Style? Say exactly what you mean, and when you have said it, be sure you have said exactly that. That is style."

All I needed to sell my book to a publishing house was a structure, a skeleton, a table of contents, but I could not come up with it. I could not mesh the narrative into the historical material so that the transitions were smooth. I had great globs of historical matter woven into a rowboat narrative, and it did not work. It will never be published, and it is a pity too, because of all that cleverness!

Reduce everything to heads and subheads and 1, 2, 3. Get into the business of outlining, but don't let it show. The skeleton must never show, any more than it does in our bodies. We clothe it with flesh, but the basic skeleton must be there.

Billy Graham preached a sermon about the rich young ruler who came to Jesus. He said he came when he was at the right age; he came in the right mood; he came to the right person; he asked the right question; he got the right answer; and he did the wrong thing. How is that for an outline?

A writer with average gifts can turn out a book, a good book, if there is a good outline, if the material is organized. A great help in organizing material is to ask, "What am I trying to say?"

Now a word about transitions. Transitions can be smooth or they can be rough. One of the most obvious transitions is a word such as "however" or "nevertheless" or "on the other hand." Instead, try to make transitions undiscernible so that the copy moves logically from one point to the next.

Keep the progression simple! Go directly to your points 1, 2, 3, after a bright introduction. The introduction, of course, is a separate thing. It should be lively; it should be catchy; it should be provocative—a grabber.

Then we move into our points, and there must be no deviation or omission. If you protest, "It is too simple and too short"—well, after you have your structure, you can drop in an illustration, something that a well-known person said, or something that you have experienced, to illustrate the point being made.

A warning here about acrostics, acronyms, and alliterations. I contend that while alliteration may be cute, it is not literature. Five peas in a pod, or seven Cs, or four Ds, are unacceptable to me. You don't see them in Scripture. I know some ministers use them all the time, and they think they are fine. But by the time I have been led down the path of *prayer, perception, purpose, perspicuity, perseverance,* I am wondering if the next two points will be *peanuts* and *popcorn.* I don't want memory helpers, I just want the gospel. I want strong meat, not alphabet soup.

A third stage in getting our article published is *follow-through.* It is one thing to grind out a piece to fill a hole, to meet a particular need; but to do a saturation job, to research a piece, to pick up the loose ends, to check out the spelling, the documentation, the permissions, bring it up to date—these are the elements that bring a sense of completeness to the article and give it a flavor of authenticity.

You say you are not an authority on the subject? One can always substantiate one's material. I am not an authority on sociology, yet I wrote a book on the evangelical social conscience. I documented everything and got by with it. It was criticized, but nobody said, "He does not know what he is talking about," because I listed my sources in the notes.

We don't have to be a living authority on a subject to write about it. Let us take an example: the ministry to the blind people of your state. Perhaps you are not the director of an institution for the blind, but you come in as an observer. You have your notebooks; you ask for the resources; you check out the literature; you get documentation. You can write the story. All you have to do is put the sentences together and have them make sense and follow the kind of outline that I have suggested.

The conclusion should relate back to the introduction and should in a subtle way summarize what has been said. And very important: make your article end strongly. And then just cut it off. That is the end. You don't have to make a rehash or a recapitulation, like, "And so we see as a result that we must go ahead and decide this," or that sort of tiresome thing. Just cut it off.

Follow-through involves more than just tidying up the loose ends. It involves building through suspense to a climax. It involves holding back a key anecdote with which to wind up the article. It involves a satisfying conclusion.

I wrote my first book when I was 22 years old, on the shores of Hilo Bay in Hawaii, under the coco palms, in the winter of 1933 and 1934. It was an account of my 17 days as a deck boy in the U.S. Merchant Marine aboard the sugar freighter *Maunalei*. I was shepherding 44 crates of chickens across the middle of the Pacific, and the chickens got out, and they insisted on walking through the feed and tipping the water cans over into it, so that I had grass growing out in the middle of the Pacific. It was a funny manuscript, but it failed to sustain the tempo, and all of a sudden it ran out of steam. I had nothing more to say. I got myself to Hawaii, and there I was, and I did not know how to cut it off or wrap it up. The literary agent said, "It is very entertaining, but it just is not going to make it." No follow-through.

We can add to our research by writing to very important people. I suggest we get as much material as we can on the subject. Build a big file. We will not use it all, but we can take a bit here and a bit there and piece it together. Get so much material you don't know what to do with it all. Sift it. Pick out the best illustrations and sew them into the article. Follow through and check out the material.

How many times have you read that while the *Titanic* was sinking the ship's orchestra played "Nearer My God to Thee"?

Well, we researched it and we found that this did not happen on the *Titanic* at all, it was the *Lusitania;* and it was not the orchestra, it was the Royal Welsh Male Chorus; and they did not play, they sang. But the hymn was right.

Make contact with the reader, organize the material, and follow through to complete the job.

7

PUTTING IN THE SPARKLE

C. S. Lewis' autobiography *Surprised by Joy* is a beautiful work. He doesn't tell us very much about himself or about God, but just enough, and then we fill in the empty spaces in our own imagination. And what he says sparkles.

The relationship between God and humankind is not a cliché and God help us if we put it into the form of a cliché. We cannot describe that relationship with expressions taken from what other people said at a Bible-conference witness hour. Every day's testimony is fresh. Every Christian writer's witness should carry its own sparkle.

Let me now give you four characteristics that will add to your writing a sparkling quality. I have said that I avoid alliterations, and it's true, but these just happen to start with S: *smoothness, suspense, subtlety,* and *shock*.

Smoothness is what we continually try to achieve in our writing. We devote precious moments to fussing about commas and semicolons. We invert clauses; we transpose adjectives; we read over passages aloud to ourselves. When we come to a point where we trip and stumble, we rework it and smooth it out.

Smoothness is a matter of practice, of muttering phrases to oneself, getting the rhythm and the alchemy of the language into one's head and heart and fingertips. We take hold of the English language and use it as a weapon. Don't let it overpower you. You are alive, and the dictionary is dead. You can control the dictionary; you can control the language; you can make it say what you want it to say. Bend it to your purposes.

Suspense is the second point. Suspense draws a person into the next paragraph to find out what happened. It means we don't take all the marbles out of our pocket at the start of the game. We hold back the agates till the end. We don't have to manufacture suspense with a trick. It can be created simply by a skillful handling of material in which we don't give away everything in the opening paragraph.

One of the old techniques of the storyteller was to say, "Now by the time I get through, you will see why he shouldn't have done that." Well, we can't be quite as open as that. We have to be more subtle than to say, "But I'm getting ahead of my story," yet that is the effect we seek to achieve. We give just a hint to create expectation, to let people know that something unusual and remarkable will be divulged later in the article, something that might be just what the reader has been watching for. This is our goal. Our Lord Jesus Christ was a master of it, and so was the apostle Paul in his famous plea in his own defense.

The third point is *subtlety*. Subtlety is the gift of presenting truth in a way that overtakes readers by surprise because they were not expecting truth; they were expecting something else. Subtle writers introduce their message in devious and interesting ways, by innuendo and inference and by nuance and by shading, and force their reader to think through the implications and arrive at their own conclusion. This is a contrast to the slab-of-granite approach, which is to be avoided in Christian literature. When we start a tract by asking, "Do you want to go to hell when you die?" we have lost our reader. Perhaps people did such things at one time when there was a dearth of literature, but they certainly don't do them today. The human mind will not be won by being overwhelmed. It will be won when it is challenged, when it is complimented, sometimes even when it is diverted.

There comes a point when we talk about sin and salvation and we don't have to be subtle any more. There comes a time when we have to hit the reader over the head, and there is no need to be mealymouthed in presenting the way of salvation, the way into the kingdom of God. Then we can call a spade a spade and a shovel a shovel; but we get there, not with a sandbag, but with a well-marshalled argument. We have been leading by a straightforward, simple, interesting, and subtle discourse into the very greatest issue of life, and we have not lost our unsaved reader along the way.

Read Paul's sermon to the Athenians in Acts 17. He speaks of God being the God of all people, and then he brings his listeners to the hard fact of the resurrection. It's beautiful the way Paul adapts his message to different audiences. When he went to Corinth, he preached Christ and him crucified, because Corinth had a different situation. Athens had an intellectual problem; Corinth had a moral problem.

Fourth, *shock.* The way I use it, shock means punch, it means vim, it means vibrancy, it means bounce, it means lift. Sometimes the only way a person can write with shock is when that person is furious. There is plenty of shock in Paul's letter to the Galatians. He does not pay many compliments. He starts out, "You stupid Galatians." That is the text. "I am shocked," he says. "It is incredible what you have been doing."

Evangelistic writing without the quality of shock is apt to wither away into sentimentality or to evaporate into boredom. We have to punch out the gospel. We can take the reader along so long, and then the quality of shock has to come through, otherwise we are not faithful to the gospel, and God help us if we are not. This is where the power comes in. We can write without this dynamic thrust, and maybe editors will print what we write, but that does not mean anyone will read it.

The hard-hitting words don't have to be violent words, just words of clarity. We can be kind, we can be winsome. Yet we will never capture the citadel of the human soul without this element of shock.

One could write a Christian novel with only one line in it about Jesus Christ dying for our sins, and yet if the novel were put out in the airport bookstands and sold to the average reader, that one line could have more effect than a dozen books of unread sermons.

Sometimes I become disturbed about a subject, and I will sit down at the machine, and righteous indignation pours out of me. I am indignant, I am scornful, and I think I will just pulverize people with what I have written. Then I go to bed. Next day I read over that lush purple passage of prose, and I overwriting? You just threw away your argument. You had a case, but you ruined it by overstating it. You act as though God could not bring in the kingdom without your sounding off."

So I just turn it upside down, and I rewrite it calmly and objectively. The indignation is still there, but it is under control. We get our point across, and people will realize that we are saying something; we are arguing with alarm but are not going up in smoke.

Shock means a Sunday punch. Have you read *The Old Man and the Sea* by Hemingway? What is the moment of truth? What is the Sunday punch? It is when the first shark appears. The man has caught the biggest tarpon that was ever seen in the Caribbean, and then the first shark hits the boat with the giant tarpon tied to it.

The Sunday punch in the story of the prodigal son is when the elder brother walks into the scene. The Sunday punch is not a trick ending. It is a dramatic development, the unexpected introduction of something new, a catalyst that changes the picture. This has been the hallmark of a good storyteller since the days of Aesop.

When I was a boy, my Scoutmaster was an immigrant from Australia; his name was Percy Shelley. He was one of the most wonderful men I ever met. He loved boys. He used to take us to Pirate's Cove in Marin County in California, and we would build a campfire and sit around the logs and look at the fire and we would say, "Shelley, tell us a story."

So he would tell us a ghost story, and we would sit listening. After I had been through such an experience once or twice, I was just half an inch off the edge of that log all the time, because I knew there was going to come a point where Shelley would say, "And suddenly . . . ." And my heart would just go *boom*. The Sunday punch. Shock us a little bit. That will make the story stand up and talk.

There is a Sunday punch in the story of the human race, because Paul tells us while we were without strength, in due time, Christ died for the ungodly. While the world lay gripped in tyranny and wickedness, God intervened and sent his Son to die for us and to take away our sin. This is the Sunday punch. This is the story that you and I have been sent to tell. It is not a dogmatic formulation, and it is not a preachment; it is a story. We are going to get farther with our stories than with anything else. We are to write this story in a new and compelling way, not to obtain personal fulfillment and self-realization, and not to justify our existence before God, but to help others to find Jesus as Savior and Lord.

8

THE SIGNIFICANCE OF WORDS

Marshall McLuhan announced that we had moved out of the age of Gutenberg into the age of television. He said that ours can no longer be considered a "linear" or reading era but rather the era of symbolism and visual images. Unfortunately, he had to write a book to declare these astonishing developments, and thereby weakened his point. The spoken word cannot eliminate the written word. Literature will be around as long as people are around; and when the last word is written, God will write it.

Words are among the most important things in the universe. When a person is unconscious, we listen first for the breathing; we wait for the eyes to open; then we listen for utterance, for speech, for words. Words mean life. "In the beginning was the Word" (John 1:1). "Heaven and earth will pass away," said Jesus, "but not my words" (Mark 13:31).

Generals of the infantry will tell us that a good battle cry is worth many platoons in combat. But a battle cry is nothing more than a slogan, and a slogan is a popular combination of words: "Fifty-four forty or fight," "Hang the Kaiser," "England, and Saint George," "I shall return." These are words, and by them people live and die.

What a beautiful gift God has given us, this gift of language! I form words, you form them, and we hear and read each other's thoughts. We catch the meaning.

Every successful craftsman is familiar with his material. The building contractor knows his concrete formulas; the carpenter knows his grades of lumber; the tailor knows his fabric; the chef knows his grades of beef and his breads and vegetables; the miner knows his rock strata; the golf champion knows his clubs.

The writer is also a craftsman, with a basic material of words. The task: to arrange those words so that they express valid ideas that others will read and grasp. If he is successful, they will pay to read, and they will agree with what he writes.

If the writer is an "idea person" as well as a "word person," he or she may influence a generation. People will hail the writer a genius. Most writers, however, are simply "word people." We draw our ideas from sources other than our own. We then couch them in our own words. For example, Christian writers draw their ideas from the Bible, which is their best source. Christian writers do not claim originality; they know the world will not be saved by innovation. Instead, Christian writers strive for interest, clarity, and truth.

The more we write, and the more use we make of words, the more familiar we become with them. We learn which words are clean and strong and which are second-grade. We come to sense what arrangements of words will create a smooth effect, what will convey suspense, what will achieve subtlety, what will please, what will depress, and what will sound the alarm.

To express yourself effectively, you do not need a large vocabulary. Abraham Lincoln did very well with a few well-chosen words. Many a writer's effectiveness is in inverse ratio to his or her working vocabulary; that is, the more words the writer uses, the worse the stuff reads. But at the same time I will never recommend writing "basic English." It is a shame to put limits on language. Properly used, a wide vocabulary can add great power to your ideas.

Words are tools. They make us pros. You may not be a success, but if you can handle words, you will never starve; and you may become a voice for God in this generation such as you never imagined. Such achievement takes work, effort, persistence, diligence, and discipline. You say, "I don't have a poetic imagination; I don't have the vocabulary; I don't have—" Just a moment. Do you have *The Synonym Finder* by Rodale? If you have it, you have all you need. Simply start to use it. That's what I mean by work.

The English language belongs to you. You don't belong to it. It is your servant, not your master. Language is a living thing, and it lives because you are using it.

Editors read manuscript after manuscript looking for interesting and exciting words and find so few. That is because most writers are lazy and won't look for a more interesting choice than the word that comes immediately to mind. Editors are grateful for any drops of color in your paragraphs. These colorful words must be appropriate; they cannot stick out too obviously; but they can do a lot for your writing. Originality and creativity do not mean discovering something new; there is nothing new under the sun. Creativity is putting old things together in a different and fresh way.

To speak of words is also to speak of style, for style is the posture we adopt in our use of words. Style is personality expressing itself by putting words together in characteristic ways.

Many writing styles have become popular in our day.

One is used by C. S. Lewis. It is chatty and informal, but never cheap. Lewis succeeded in putting profound truths into everyday language and making them seem deceptively simple. Our Lord Jesus Christ, of course, also exercised this gift. Such a style is easy to read and easy to understand, and is a great relief from the textbooks.

Another popular style is reportorial and was introduced into literature by Ernest Hemingway. It involves a use of terse understatement, with heavy emphasis on technical knowledge. It seems to carry the ring of authenticity. Tell it the way it is, without editorial comment. Let readers draw their own conclusions from the facts.

Another popular style, and I regret to say it seems to be increasingly popular, is the prejudicial. Many contemporary writers no longer are content to tell it as it is; they report on the basis of their prejudices and biases. They evaluate in terms of their own preconceived notions, advocatory or adversative. For them the world is a stage, and they are reviewing the play—or more likely, they are panning it.

Still another popular style is whimsy. Humorous writing is in great demand. Art Buchwald and Erma Bombeck are contemporaries; Robert Benchley, Dorothy Sayers, Will Rogers are earlier stylists of this type. Christian humorists would find a ready market today, but they are rare birds.

THE SIGNIFICANCE OF WORDS

There are also unpopular writing styles, and unfortunately, they still have their proponents in religious circles.

One such style is the hard-sell. It is an evangelical favorite.

Then there is the gee-whiz school. It gives us excitement no end. We are breathless! So we stop reading.

Still another unpopular style is the pious overkill: sweet, sticky, cloying religious language, clichés galore, heart throbs of yesteryear. Unfortunately, some people still like it and pay to read it.

Now here are some ideas for you to consider in handling the words of a sentence. Notice I didn't say "Here are some *tips*," or, "Here are some *suggestions.*" Why not? Because I am not giving tips; I am helping to circulate ideas. You are not my pupil; you are my fellow writer. It is a fine distinction, but the right word will convey it. I had to go to the dictionary to find it.

1. Use active verbs instead of passive. Instead of saying, "Bertrand was bitten by a snake," or "Bertrand suffered a snake bite," or "Bert was snake-bit," turn it around: "A snake bit Bertrand."

2. Eliminate unnecessary adverbs and adjectives. To understand what I mean, read the short story that changed the whole tenor of North American literature, "The Killers" by Ernest Hemingway. I should say parenthetically here that adverbs and adjectives do have their place, as will be seen in a moment.

3. Avoid label words such as "liberal" and "fundamentalist." Avoid overworked color words such as "ghastly," "horrible," "beastly," and also "terrific," "smashing," "tremendous." My wife used to talk about city traffic giving her a heart attack. Later she toned it down and said she was having a "cardiac arrest." Much more interesting.

4. Use a synonym finder when you are having trouble with a word—and when you are not having trouble. Examples: "asinine" to "foolish," "rejoiced" to "exulted."

5. Avoid using "I" too often in a testimony or in anything else.

6. Strive for understatement. In an age of superlatives, understatement will not fail to attract attention if it is applied with humor. British humor is delightful because it is droll, straight-faced, and understated.

7. Avoid professional jargon. American educational jargon includes expressions like "in terms of," "frames of reference," "extrapolated," and "phased out." Watch for these traps. Some jargon is permissible, in small doses, but the secret is to avoid repetition.

8. Don't play obvious games with words. In "The Raven" Poe described "the silken, sad, uncertain rustling of each purple curtain." It was supposed to convey the wind blowing a curtain, but it didn't come off because it was too obvious. Onomatopoeia must be treated very delicately.

I plead not for the elimination of adjectives but for their judicious and sparing use.

As for adverbs, here is an example of how they can be used in abundance with effectiveness:

> May I seek to live this day quietly, easily,
> leaning on your mighty strength trustfully,
>   restfully,
> meeting others in the path peacefully, joyously,
> waiting for your will's unfolding patiently,
>   serenely,
> facing what tomorrow brings confidently,
>   courageously.

The chief reason our material is not being accepted as we wish it to be is not because our ideas are erroneous, not because our motivation is suspect, not because our illustrations are weak or our logic faulty. It is simply because of what we do with words—words—words. When we clothe those words with flesh, they come and dwell among us and gladden our existence.

9

THE EFFECTIVE USE OF WORDS

A few years ago I tried to find out which passage of Martin Luther's introduction to the letter to the Romans John Wesley was listening to when he felt his heart "strangely warmed." I went to the library of Augsburg College in Minneapolis and examined three translations, and they were all so different that I decided to tackle the original German. To my astonishment, the translations were only pale copies of the original; Luther's German proved to be rich, strong, earthy, and gripping, but the English equivalents were flat words, of Latin derivation, so that what came out of Luther in power ended up reading like the minutes of the Royal Botanical Society.

Had I to choose, I would much rather read articles that used sharp, vibrant words in the wrong sense, than articles that used dull words in the right sense. Shakespeare was above all other things a master of words—not that his vocabulary was so extensive, but he chose his words to convey vivid impressions. He was a word painter. So was Abraham Lincoln. And so can you be, if you take the trouble.

This mastery of words does not require genius; it does require time. It is a matter of pausing five seconds before you write that key word, to see whether you can substitute a better one. When we are dealing with Anglo-Saxon derivatives, English can be a strong, almost brutal language, with tremendous expressiveness. This Teutonic element is what enraptured the Germans with Shakespeare; they look on him as their own and claim the English don't understand him.

But I do not wish to decry the Norman and Latin elements in the English language, which add tremendously to its variety, beauty, and flexibility. One can say all manner of things in English that simply cannot be expressed in French or German. That is one reason that English is fast becoming the most popular language around the world, after the native tongue.

To show what I mean by variety and expressiveness, I will ask you to play a game with me. I want you to try to find a better word for the one I use. I want a word that is more specific, more colorful, more descriptive, more interesting. I will give you some examples:

A bird [chickadee] perched on the clothesline.
He drove up in a car [slightly battered Plymouth].
A tree [Ponderosa pine] stood in the yard.
The house had a basement [downstairs workshop].
A sidewalk [flagstones] led to the house.
He worked in New York City [Manhattan].
For a hobby he raised chickens [Leghorns].

Pick up the jargon that people use around their work. Here is one of the best ways to add authenticity to writing. You will discover that the airlines refer not to their "planes" but to their "equipment"; the Coca-Cola salesman refers not to his "juice" but to his "merchandise"; the baseball pitcher does not talk about his "slowball" and his "curve," but about his "change-up" and his "slider."

In the church there are also distinctions. Whom the Episcopalians call a priest, the Pentecostals call a minister, and the Lutherans a pastor. Baptists speak of parsonages and ordinances; the Presbyterians, of manses and sacraments.

Develop an accurate, discriminatory feeling for words. Become friendly with words. New words can be tremendously exciting companions. Words are also great fun. People go into stitches over words. *My Fair Lady*, the adaptation of Shaw's *Pygmalion*, was built on the way people use words. Dickens is noted for the way his characters in the *Pickwick Papers* manhandled ordinary words. If you would like to write about your own childhood, reproduce the exact expressions that your folks used—nothing phony, nothing corny, just the real thing. Those expressions alone could sell your article.

Now, having heard all this, you are faced with the immediate problem of writing an article. You know what you want to say, but you're afraid that after you have put it all down with a great deal of effort, no one will be interested. But just for a moment come and sit behind the editor's desk and consider a dilemma. The magazine has a circulation problem. The editor cannot go out and hustle subscriptions to stay afloat. There is only one thing to do, and that is to make the pages just as interesting and polished and sparkling as possible.

This may take a considerable amount of tinkering with your copy, but the editors are willing to do it if they have the time. They do not expect your manuscript to be perfect. They are willing to touch it up but do not want to rewrite it for you. If the magazine is a weekly, it may be forced to use your stuff as it is. And that is just what is wrong with so much of our Christian literature.

Here is an article that is loaded with nuclear warheads. It is revolutionary in content, and it coins a new idea that is so arresting that the idea was picked up and made the basis for a lead article in the religion section of *Time* magazine. Yet the article is not well put together. It is prosaic, and its lead is so dull that one wonders whether anyone under 50 would bother to read it. It begins by saying, "The purpose of this article is to suggest that each of the major Protestant denominations could wisely establish as an integral part of its theological educational system a new type of theological seminary."

Let's pause for a moment to examine this article. There is obviously more here than reporting or observing. A fresh idea is involved, something creative. So we begin to read, and we run into this lead sentence. The word *theological* is used twice. Worse yet, the author gives away the show. There is no suspense, no build-up. The page is flat reading, without illustration. The author does say some things of great interest, if only we had the patience to pick our way over the rocky moraine of unpleasant, dull, heavy words.

Our task is to find new ways of stating scriptural truths, vividly, imaginatively, compellingly. We need a language breakthrough by a band of men and women writers who will give the world a 20th-century Christian vocabulary that is as quick and powerful and sharp and piercing as that of the first-century church.

Consider how effective individual words can be in our titles. Here are three secular titles that arrested the attention of the public a few years ago:

Ten Days That Shook the World. Notice the one-syllable words.

Why Johnny Can't Read. This could be adapted for Christian use: an article could be entitled, "Why VBS Is Dying." Such shock technique should be used sparingly, but it should be used.

I Was a Teen-age Werewolf. This writer combined two popular concepts, youth and horror, to make a fortune. Titles are important.

Finally, a couple of choice and original words at the end of your article will provide a fillip or a snap that will be just what you need to get your piece off Dismal Hill and onto the Highway of Hope. It could be an apt quote in the closing sentence from Winston Churchill or Omar Bradley or Josh Billings or Billy Graham or Barry Goldwater or Martin Luther King or Paul of Tarsus. Even one word might bring it off. Don't drift off into a "something ought to be done" line or a pointless "recap" of what you have already said. Use the last sentence to give the impact of a springboard, to start readers thinking on their own.

Now go back to that particular article you have drafted and are anxious about. Do a little dreaming. Imagine you are trying to catch the attention of an editor who is sitting in a chair, being pressed on all sides by people who want him to read what they have in their hands. You must attract his attention. What will you do? You realize that you haven't stated it as forcefully as you might, so you take it back and rewrite it, making it more urgent. You think of little ways to catch his attention. You cater to his prejudices. You try to think his thoughts—you anticipate his needs—for somehow you have to get that paper into his hand. By now you have lost your natural reticence; you have become quite bold; you are willing to try any literary device that will work.

So you push your piece of writing at the editor, and it has cockleburrs sticking all over it, and what happens? He reads it. Congratulations! You have just sold a story to an editor who did not have the least intention, when he picked up your manuscript, of spending more than 20 seconds on it. And you did it with words that screamed like fire engines and bounced like golf balls and went rat-tat-tat like woodpeckers. But when you talked about God, it was as the voice of many waters.

You see, you can put words together. You can become a voice for God in this generation. Who made the greatest impact in the 20th century for Christ in the English language? Was it a preacher? No, it was a man who sat in a stark study in Magdalen College in Oxford, England, and his name was C. S. Lewis. This man, who lived a simple, uneventful life, said more, did more, influenced more people high and low around the world than any preacher. C. S. Lewis made a tremendous impression for Jesus Christ. Why? Because he could use words.

10

THE LIGHT TOUCH

The light touch is an approach to Christian literature that seeks to make it readable. It moves on the premise that unless prose is interesting, it is not worth perusing and therefore not worth writing. One secret of the light touch is that it brings out the ironies and incongruities in a situation. I believe that the incongruities of existence can be used for a double purpose: to evoke a bit of humor and to lead the reader on to faith. Both humor and faith deal with life's paradoxes. Laughter and trust are the ways in which we Christians reconcile ourselves to the great irreconcilable mysteries. Laughter tells us that it is a crazy, ridiculous, preposterous world. We had better learn to laugh, or we shall find it impossible to live in it. Trust places those mysteries ultimately in the hands of a sovereign God.

The light touch that I am proposing to you is an English approach, by and large. Excellent examples are the novels of

Jane Austen and Anthony Trollope. One finds something similar in the French writers—Voltaire, de Maupassant, Anatole France, Sartre—but it always has a bitter edge. It is not so characteristic of German writing, which leans toward the heavy side. Slavic literature knows nothing of it, from Tolstoy to Gorky to Pasternak. Americans engage in a great deal of writing in the light vein, but our humor tends to be too contrived. Like Art Buchwald, we set out to do a funny piece. Buchwald's pieces can be very funny, but I am not speaking of funny pieces. I am speaking of a spirit that informs the whole, even much of the strong writing. I would say the late Halford Luccock is one of the better examples of the light American touch. Like G. K. Chesterton, R. H. Tawney, George Bernard Shaw, Dorothy Sayers, and C. S. Lewis, he wrote jocularly but with restraint. More recently Bob Friedman has written a gem, *What's a Nice Jewish Boy Like You Doing in the First Baptist Church?*

If you can master this touch, I am confident that it will speed you on your way, and that it will help market your articles quickly.

That is not all it will do! My wife, Winola, wrote an article for the British Christian weekly, *The Life of Faith*. She described how she went into an antique shop and looked over an attractive jug, but resisted the temptation to buy it. Then she began witnessing to the proprietress, asking her if she had been to Earls Court to the Crusade that Billy Graham was holding there at that time. The woman had not. My wife asked if she would like some tickets. The woman would be delighted. My wife gave her the tickets, said good-bye and left. But when she wrote the story Winola put it this way: "'Good-bye,' I said, eyeing the jug for the last time."

You would not believe it, but when the article appeared, a woman subscriber read it, telephoned Winola, said what a pity she did not buy the jug, bought a whole suitcase full of antiques to give to the wives of members of the Billy Graham team, and then made a contribution to the Crusade!

What did the addition of those words do? It revealed the author as a human being, tempted in all points like the rest of us. This is the light touch. If you exhibit it in your writing, instead of the proud, holier-than-thou attitude or the listen-to-teacher maxims that pervade most of our religious literature, editors will be surprised and amazed. They may even go into shock. Your writing will be no less earnest for being honest, but it will be more acceptable. Your writing will be more suggestive and less exhaustive. People will decide that they like the way you put things, and once they have decided that, you have a style. You are on your way.

Now, what are the qualities and characteristics of the light touch? First, it betrays a healthy digestion. If a man can see the whimsical side of life, we do not assume that he has no troubles; we feel that he has managed to rise above them. The writer who can do this can keep bile and dyspepsia from coming out on paper, no matter what the subject matter. And the reader unconsciously thinks, "The world has not got this person down. How come? Maybe I can learn something from him."

Second, the light touch has personal objectivity. The classic subject, of course, is a person's own inconsistencies and foibles. This can be overdone; we can exploit ourselves until people are sick of reading about us. But true personal objectivity is not self-obsession. It is simply a matter of refusing to take ourselves too seriously, even in Christian writing. Usually when Christians write, their subject matter is serious. They are talking about their Lord. The treasure is amethyst and sapphire and onyx, but remember that the vessel is earthen; that is to say, it is made of clay and mud.

I do not mean that the Christian should forget about holiness and set out to become more worldly than the world. There is nothing more pitiful than a Christian trying to "identify" with the world by imitating it. It certainly does not impress unbelievers. The greatest saints were nothing but honest men and women with faith. They were great partly because they were willing to admit their humanity.

Third, the light touch is a writing tool. It can be used as a device or technique to make a point. Suppose you wish to interest your reader in a serious discussion of a fairly heavy subject—the need, let us say, for a new kind of Sunday-school curriculum. To read a ponderous piece of literature requires effort. People are increasingly reluctant to put forth the effort. A light touch will carry readers into a discussion without strain; they will find your opening paragraph rather engaging, and they will go along with you to see if there are any more like it. If you have further touches along the way—and you should, as any successful lecturer will tell you—then the curse of tedium will be taken off your article, and people will decide that not only do you have something to say, as a Christian should, but you say it well.

Fourth, the light touch is Scripturally warranted. The person to whom the Bible is a closed book thinks of it as a series of thou-shalt-nots and list of begats and a collection of dire threatenings. But the light touch can be found in many parts of the Bible: in Genesis, in the books of Samuel and Kings, in the Psalms and Proverbs, in Jonah, and of course in the

Gospels, particularly in the stories and parables of Jesus. I suggest that in your own Bible reading, you mark such passages with a colored pencil.

Now it is time to ask how one goes about learning to acquire and use the light touch. So many of us in our private conversations are full of little dashes of humor, but when we sit down to write, we freeze. We say we can't think of a thing. We think we are on display, so we try to put our best foot forward. That is another way of describing an ego trip. I would suggest that perhaps we ought to put our worst foot forward. It belongs to us too. But let's say just what we mean.

1. *Exploit every bit of humor that there is in a situation*—any situation. You were on your way home from downtown, the buses were on strike, you waited for a taxi, it started to rain, you had just come from the beauty parlor, the umbrella wouldn't work, your clothes began to shrink—give it everything you have.

2. *Let your natural sense of drama take over.* Tell it as you would over the telephone, or to a friend over a cup of coffee. Build up the suspense. If you have to rearrange the facts in order to make it a first-class story, then put it in third person and go to it.

3. *Combine opposites.* When it is properly done, this is an effective method of producing a chuckle. And a chuckle means you have readers! I remember hearing a cowboy singing on the radio. He twanged away about all his tragic experiences: his horse stepped into a badger hole, someone set fire to the bunkhouse, his sweetheart deserted him, the drought ruined the range, the herd of cattle died, the foreman let him go, and then he added, "Now I'm getting dandruff." When World War II broke out, a friend of mine in Alaska said, "Pete writes

from Idaho and says he's so discouraged by world conditions that he's not even going to cut his lawn." Call it the law of lessened effect, or a combination of opposites.

4. Couch what you say in descriptive language. The light touch depends a good deal on forsaking the old clichés and the drab adjectives and tiresome adverbs that we use over and over again in our writing. The light touch comes by practice. It calls for a daily stint. Look around you. There is a great deal of comical material in connection with the stories others can tell you. Or take church. Toy with this subject for a moment: "How our house gets ready for church." Describe how you lay in bed Sunday morning and planned it all out, just how things would go, and then you got up and—well, it just didn't work out that way. The first thing that happened was—and you take it from there. Make it vivid, even flamboyant. If you need any encouragement, read the Gospels. Our Lord used extremely colorful language: "whited sepulchres," "gnashing of teeth," "that fox."

Now, the first draft of your writing will hardly amount to more than wild notes and jottings, put down hurriedly, perhaps even in suppressed excitement and laughter. Don't worry about style, about grammar, about anything. Just get it down. Let it bubble over. That process will provide the raw material that you can build on later.

The second draft will show the first signs of something taking shape and will include a lot of embellishment of what you wrote first.

Then the third draft gets down to something that you are seriously considering submitting to an editor. At this point I believe it is ready to be looked over by someone else with a critical eye.

Christians are, as I have suggested, supremely qualified to write in the vein of lightness. After all, it is a matter of vast relief to know that our burden of sin has been lifted, that we are forgiven, that our salvation is sure. It is enough to make anyone lighthearted. The distinguished American psychologist, Gordon W. Allport, has written, "A case might be made for the potentially superior humor of the religious person who has settled once and for all what things are of ultimate value, sacred and untouchable. For then nothing else in the world need be taken seriously."[3] That being the case, what a distortion of truth and reality it is when the claim is made, as it sometimes is, that "Christianity smothers laughter"!

The world as we know it becomes increasingly complex; ours is not a very pleasant century, and many people have reacted to it by becoming bitter realists who are unwilling to take anything on faith. Romance, idealism, nobility—these are forgotten words. Many of today's writers are angry young men and women. Their products are soiled with filth, brutality, desperation, and unbelief.

It is possible that the only light and pleasantly readable literature of the 1980s and 1990s will come from believers who face the future with confidence, no matter what the human prospect. It is possible that we shall become the people who hold the literary world together. The challenge is ours.

11

THE STRONG TOUCH

What is the strong touch? I can think of no better description than the one contained in Matthew's gospel: "He taught as one who had authority" (7:29). The strong touch is the touch of the master, the mark of authenticity, the touch of an author who, while not infallible, knows what he or she is talking about, and who is acquainted with the divine element of truth behind the subject at hand.

The strong touch is the touch of a strong person, and you can be that person.

Let us start by saying that the surest way to bring that touch to your writing is to plant in it liberally the good seed of the gospel. We have nothing else to compare with Jesus, nothing else in our quiver as powerful and significant. Our copy can be dead—just a lot of words strung one after another, cold and lifeless. Then we begin to move into what the poet Masefield called "the burning cataracts of Christ," and our machines begin to hum and purr.

So much average Christian writing never quite gets around to the law and the gospel. It buzzes about the outside petals but never crawls into the flower. It never tells us that the world is lost without God; that ours is a planet in revolt; that man was created in the image of God, but rebelled, and stands alienated today from God and humanity and corrupted by sin. Then the good news: that God has reconciled the world to himself through the life, death, and resurrection of Jesus Christ. By his Spirit we are reunited with God and with one another, and set free from the bondage of sin and death.

You and I don't have to go into our favorite three points or four points or 14 points of the faith every time we write a devotional; leave that to the theologians. It is an unfortunate fact that theological writers (at least the modern variety) do not win many of their readers to Christ. But novelists like Charles Williams can, and do. Dramatists like Dorothy Sayers can, and do. Poets like John Donne can, and do. Theology is important, but for a working writer what is vital is not acquaintance with all the fine points of dogma; rather it is the ability to take a basic, elementary, solid grasp of gospel truth and make use of it in writing. It has to be acceptable to the reader, of course; but that does not mean it cannot be aggressive.

I once read a book by one of those fellow-travelers who flirt with the edges of the gospel. The writer was saying, "You can be the person you like, if you dare." He was tossing in bits of psychology and group-think and summer-camp inspiration; but it was weak tea. It had no New Testament stinger in it, no doctrine of sin. It lacked the strong touch of a supernatural God wrestling with people who need to be saved from hell. Television abounds in such saccharine pap.

When I suggest that you do not need a three-year course in systematic theology, I am not implying that the strong touch is a mark of ignorance. The gospel of Jesus Christ has a way of imparting wisdom even to those who are lacking in erudition. I think of a lay preacher like Billy Bray, the Cornish miner, or Pecos Higgins, the Arizona cowboy poet. I would pit these men in debate against an existentialist philosopher any time. The Holy Spirit has given gifts to many a humble believer that some of the greatest intellectuals yearn to have.

The gospel of Jesus Christ can make writing interesting and strong. There will always be a concurrent need for literary artistry, for timing, for suspense, for descriptive setting, for characterization, for a dexterous use of words. But in the end it is the glad word of salvation that carries the knockout blow.

You can work it into a golf story. You can splice it into a murder mystery. You can use it to interpret a historical study. You can call on it to suffuse a poem with inspiration. You can employ it in one way or another in a devotional diary, a Christmas play, a biography, a testimony, a church article. Wedge it in! Remember that the word *preach* is related to the Greek word *euangelion*. And that means "to proclaim the glad tidings." As Christian writers that is what we are called to do, whatever the form our writing takes. For we are unashamedly propagandists, out to win the world for Christ, not through a distortion of the truth but through the proclamation of the truth. For us to write, therefore, is to preach, to announce the glad tidings.

Well, then, do we have to insert John 3 or Romans 7 or Ephesians 2 every time we slip a fresh sheet into our machine? By no means. Let's hope we can be a little more ingenious than that. But somewhere along the way our faith has to shine through. Emil Brunner says of us ordinary Christians that there is something which "from love and in love we are to do to our neighbor in accordance with the will of the Creator and the Redeemer."[4] He adds, "In cooperation we are to do what everyone does, and we are also to act differently from others." How? "At the right time and place," says Brunner, "the ordinary Christian will say something amazing, something which does not simply belong to the subject in hand, something unexpected, about God and eternal things, something which, just because it is said at an unusual time and in an unusual way, will have more demonstrative, attractive, and awakening power than the majority of sermons."

That is our challenge as Christian writers. I am assuming of course that you are in favor of the gospel. Many writers are not. If they go into the subject of "religion," it is to describe their revolt against the Christianity of their youth, their loathing of the church's discipline, their disillusionment with its so-called professors. So many contemporary authors use their books as a catharsis to explain and justify their flight from God. We, on the other hand, write to establish faith in God and in his gospel.

As Christian writers we have a responsibility to tell the whole truth, the good as well as the bad. Imagine the psalmist spending all his time complaining that the temple was too cold, and the incense too thick, and the marble slabs too hard on his knees! He would never have had time or energy to write Psalm 100, or 139, or 150. Suppose Luke had spent his time reporting the things Paul "failed to touch on" in his sermons in Asia Minor. I doubt if we would be reading the book of Acts for devotions today.

Here are a few practical ways in which you can make the strong touch the hallmark of your own writing product. First, tackle the great issues. I know a writer who has published a good many casual pieces—good, mind you, but she would be categorized as a middleweight. Then one day she wrote on assignment a study of Dante to commemorate the 700th anniversary of his birth. I would say that Dante was a magnificent subject.

The great issues should be our meat and drink. Consider the subject of true love. We need to keep alive the flame of love in literature. The whole concept is disappearing from our culture and art forms. What is true love? Don't ask Freud. Don't ask Bertrand Russell. Don't ask Ian Fleming. You are the one to be asked, and you are the one to give the answer.

Consider the subject of hope. If you cannot get hope into your writing, then you might as well trade in your word processor for a color TV set. You must give us hope. We need you to tell us that Christianity works; that it issues in victorious, fruitful Christian living, no matter what the problem, no matter how desperate the situation; and that after death things get better yet.

Second, get hold of something believable. Once and for all, let's get our Christian writing out of the 19th century. Other people can hold back the times, but you cannot afford to. Your place is out front, beckoning. The old landmarks that Jeremiah warned us to observe, the old paths that he told us to walk in, they are out in front, too. God does not change; he is the eternal contemporary.

One radiant statement by a believer may well leave the modern cynic speechless. "One thing I know—that whereas I was blind, now I see"—how do you answer that?

Get this kind of believability into your writing. Don't just write about your mother's faith; write about your daughter's faith. We can't remember what your mother had to face, but we have an idea as to what your daughter is going through. Your mother probably may have tried to find some answer to *Main Street,* but your daughter is faced with *Cosmopolitan* magazine and worse. Make it believable for today.

Third, your writing will be more likely to carry a strong touch if you major in clarity. Confused writing is the hallmark of our day. Ernst Kirschten, editorial writer for the St. Louis *Post-Dispatch,* says, "Write not that you may be understood, but that you cannot be misunderstood." I do not imply that one's whole thesis has to be set forth in the opening paragraphs. Let it develop naturally, but make it clear that you know what you are writing about. If two sides of a subject are called for, present them lucidly and honestly, so that the issues are clear and readers can make up their own minds.

Fourth, avoid the commonplace. An editor once told me that he deliberately used second-quality material on the back page of his paper, and paid half the usual rate for it. I think this is a parable of what is wrong with Christian literature. We are deluged with second-rate stuff. There is absolutely no excuse for it. We have the grandest theme in the world, one that has produced the Psalms, the poetry of Milton, the sermons of Spurgeon. We do not intend just to jack up the level of fillers and youth-club testimonies. We are pointing you right to the top.

Fifth, follow the natural lines of your interest and stick to them. If it be children's writing, work at it. Let that be your forte, your vocation. Develop it. Grow in it. Exactly the same could be said for writing of Sunday-school curriculum, or story papers, or interviews, or social-problem articles, or biographies, or poetry, or drama, or whatever the field. Versatility is good, but too much versatility can keep the strong touch out of your writing.

Specialization does not really restrict the writer, any more than a study of the gospel of John restricts the searcher after truth. You master your field; then you wake up one day to realize that some of the principles you have learned apply to other fields as well. But you learned your apprenticeship in this one groove.

Finally, I would say that strength can be added to your writing by a judicious use of documentation. We should have the standard reference books at our elbow. A good bibliography is always appreciated. We need to see that our statistics are accurate and our sources are reliable.

I thank God for what has been written about the gospel and what will be written. If, in the months ahead, people begin talking about a new "voice" from some corner of the Christian world, the chances are it will not be a "voice" at all. It will be the hum of a writing machine as some Christian sits down to share the good news of Jesus Christ and his saving power. And with the help of the printers and binders and publishers and distributors and bookstore owners, that good news will go out to bless men and women everywhere, just as the letters of Paul gave courage and hope to the Christians of 2000 years ago, and have done so ever since, to the praise and glory of Jesus' name.

12

THE WRITER AND THE BIBLE

Some people, wrote Andrew Lang, use statistics the way a drunk uses a lamppost—not for illumination but for support. Substitute the word "Scripture" for statistics and you have separated the amateur writers from the professionals. Nothing shows us up so obviously to the non-Christian as the way we quote the Bible. Nothing betrays our expertise more surely than our handling of Holy Writ.

If you are planning to submit to a Christian publication and pad your copy with generous interpolations of the Bible in every paragraph, you can be reasonably sure no one will read it. On the other hand, if you ignore the use of Scripture altogether, many Christian readers will wonder why you bothered to write at all.

The task calls for an artistic and discriminating touch. If we can drop encouraging, provocative bits of God's Word into our manuscript, we may whet the reader's appetite for more. But too often we wheel up our biggest cannons and fire a salvo of Bible texts at our readers, determined to bludgeon them into surrender. Instead, they disappear.

Jesus said, "Every scribe discipled into the kingdom of the heavens is like a master of a house who brings forth out of his treasure the new and the old" (Matt. 13:52, author's translation). How exquisitely put! God's trained writers, he says, draw on their experience to provide an adept mixture of the contemporary and the ancient, the latest popular phrasing and the wisdom of the ages.

By making use of the appropriate verse at the right time we give meat, strength, and ballast to what we write. What a thrilling way to employ one's talents! We enlighten our discussion by placing it against a backdrop of truth. The context is everything. The challenge to use the Bible in our writing is so great, the opportunities are so many, and the scope of Scripture is so vast, I can only hint at some of the ways open to us.

1. *Telling a Bible story.* In using such a narrative, is poetic license acceptable? That depends on how it is done. The secret, of course, is to use modern colloquial language, a technique that is quite familiar but is seldom executed well. I once heard a veteran preacher describe Nathan's denunciation of King David over his adultery with Uriah's wife, Bathsheba (2 Samuel 12). What the King James Version gives us is the prophet's thundering, "Thou art the man!" What the preacher gave us was, "Keep your shirt on, big boy! It's you!" That's on a level with the man who preached on Naaman the Syrian's encounter with the prophet Elisha (2 Kings 5) and called his sermon, "Seven Ducks in Muddy Water."

More apt was the comment of the little Dutch girl, who, during World War II, was asked to tell the story of the good Samaritan. She said, "The thieves waylaid the traveler and beat him, and took away his money and his clothes and all his ration books!" Billy Graham has a gift for updating stories about Jesus. One of his more graphic messages describes Jesus' temptation in the desert as a three-round boxing match between Jesus and Satan, with angels and demons in the cheering sections.

When we tell a Bible story and make it come alive, using embellishments that enhance rather than distort the truth, we are employing the most effective means possible of illustrating God's truth. And isn't that why we are writing?

2. *Explaining the Bible's teaching.* It may seem that Bible studies are endless, ubiquitous, and tiresome, but they don't need to be. What more satisfying activity does life offer than feeding on God's Word? Bible studies can be fresh, well written, and interesting. The author does not need a linguistic or scholarly background, but must know the subject. Publishers are constantly on the look for manuscripts that will help readers to understand the Bible by discovering for themselves what it teaches. The writer's need is to find a "handle," an approach that makes sense and suits both the text and the spiritual climate of the day.

Charles Allen wrote a little volume about Psalm 23 and called it *God's Psychiatry*. It sold a million copies. The Bible contains many small veins that yield rich spiritual ore to the excavator who is willing to dig: the Ten Commandments, the stories of Jacob, Joseph, Gideon, Micaiah, Elijah, the parables, 1 Corinthians 13, Galatians 6, and so on. My first published work, *The Cross on the Mountain*, in 1959, aimed to find the cross of Jesus in each of his Beatitudes in the Sermon on the Mount.

3. Illustrating a Bible truth. The metaphors of the Bible are based on the environment of the ancient Mediterranean coast and Fertile Crescent regions. We need to translate those metaphors into our own thought world before we can fully grasp their impact. It is the most imaginative fun in the world and makes for highly instructive teaching. Here is a sermon preached by Dr. John A. Huffman Jr., a master of the contemporary American pulpit:

> Come with me to the Rusty Pelican Restaurant in Key Biscayne, Florida. We drive along our boulevard of palm trees over the Bear Cut bridge, past the Marine stadium, taking a right turn to this tiny peninsula jutting into Biscayne Bay. Doormen escort us from our car into opulent tropical surroundings. The hostess takes us to our table located next to a picture window. Rigging ropes and long-boat oars form a unique curtain behind us. Our romantic surroundings are illuminated by flickering candlelight and the soft hues of the distant Miami skyline.
>
> Together we study our menus. Two of us order lobster-and-steak combinations. One orders prime rib. And you? No, the waiter doesn't hear you correctly. What was that you ordered? One Playtex bottle with a sterilized nipple, filled with warm milk? We can't believe it! But you're serious. You insist on having it. And all evening you sit there nursing it as we enjoy our soup course, salad plate, main entrée and delicious dessert accompanied by coffee.
>
> Ridiculous. Yet in just that way many of us live our Christian faith. We remain perpetual infants, sucking at spiritual bottles, passing up the prime cuts offered to us.[5]

Do you know the text Dr. Huffman was illustrating? "We have much to say about this, but it is hard to explain because you are slow to learn. In fact, though by this time you ought to be teachers, you need someone to teach you the elementary truths of God's Word all over again. You need milk, not solid food! Anyone who lives on milk, being still an infant, is not acquainted with the teaching about righteousness. But solid food is for the mature, who by constant use have trained themselves to distinguish good from evil" (Heb. 5:11-14).

4. *Exploring Bible words.* A favorite practice of the popular 19th-century American evangelist Dwight L. Moody was to take a single word and trace it through the Bible with a concordance. His preaching, stenographically recorded, still reads beautifully. Among Moody's published sermons may be found messages on "Love," "Grace," "Faith," "Trust," "Heaven," "Compassion," "Repentance," and even "Come!" and "Behold!"

Many other words in the Old and New Testaments need such development. No aspect of Bible teaching is more fascinating than word study. Books on the subject are available in any Christian bookstore. When we dig into Bible meanings, we draw close to truth. The field is wide open to Christian writers, and they receive the biggest blessing of all!

5. *Treatment of Bible subjects.* Originality is needed in this field, because many of the traditional Bible subjects have been exposed to overkill. The ark of Noah, Jonah and the whale, David and Goliath, the vision of Isaiah, the parable of the prodigal son, and the cleansing of the temple have become well worn not by repetitiveness so much as by triteness.

If we would write about sexual sin, why not forego David and Bathsheba and take as an illustration the story of Amnon and Tamar? If we are writing about women, instead of Mary the mother of Jesus or Mary Magdalene, why not Deborah? Why not the three women ancestors of Jesus who were of low repute? Or the daughters of Zelophehad, or the daughters of Philip?

One of the most discussed Bible subjects of our day is the Holy Spirit. Despite the spate of books, many people are still puzzled as to what the Bible says about him. Who is the Holy Spirit? What are his attributes? Where do we find the attestations of the Holy Spirit in Scripture and in the world today?

Some people are interested in the dimensions of the Jerusalem temple and the thickness of Jericho's walls, but many more are interested in the subject of the deeper life and holiness—the inner message of the Bible. When we tackle a great subject, we rise to it. And believe it or not, publishers, too, are interested.

6. *Defending the faith.* Charles Spurgeon once exclaimed, "Defend the Bible? I would sooner defend a lion!" He was right; the Bible is its own best defense. Yet the apostle Paul declared that he was "put here for the defense of the gospel" (Phil. 1:16). What did he mean? What is the difference? An article is needed to explain.

Paul wrote to the Corinthians of the danger of handling the Word of God deceitfully and thereby corrupting its meaning. Where are the rocks and shoals of corruption to be avoided today? Let us not dwell on controversies involving doctrine; let's just think about our posture and style as writers. Do we *have* to be belligerent, to say, in effect, "Take it or leave it; we're right and everybody else is wrong"? What the Bible says is, "Let God be true, and every man a liar" (Rom. 3:4), which is quite a different thing.

If a fierce defense of the Bible is undesirable, a eulogy may, by itself, be worse. Just to write glowingly about the Holy Book, to venerate it, to point out its magnificent properties and universal influence without challenging the reader to confront its message personally, is poor fare unless it is balanced.

Far better to let the Word of God prove itself. Take as a subject a psalm, a sermon of Peter, or some other portion of Scripture and show how it carries its own intrinsic authority. As the Lord himself has said, "My word . . . will not return to me empty" (Isa. 55:11).

7. *Using the Bible in a written witness.* What has the Bible done for you? It may seem irrelevant, if not preposterous, but that is what the reader would be interested in knowing. No testimony is worth its salt unless it refers to Scripture. In fact, unless the Bible comes to life in the personal testimony of a Christian, the testimony itself is suspect.

Which verse made an impression on you when you were an unbeliever? Which verse won you to believing faith? The element of mystery and speculation is always present with the reader: *maybe it will do for me what it did for you.* Even when the testimony itself leaves the reader cold, the scripture verse may send a rapier into the reader's heart. Was it a word of joy? A word of command? A word of judgment? A word out of context? The reader is not choosy, but wants to know what it was, how it affected you, and why it affected you as it did.

I have often thought a great book could be written that brought together the Bible texts that have influenced famous people and turned the tide of history at important times of crisis.

8. *Poetic use of Scripture.* The use of Scripture can do marvels for a poem. I would love to read a discussion of the use of the Bible by well-known poets: Coleridge, Browning, T. S. Eliot, Robert Frost. Here is a fascinating quatrain from Francis Thompson's poem, "The Kingdom of God":

> But (when so sad thou canst not sadder)
> Cry;—and upon thy so sore loss
> Shall shine the traffic of Jacob's ladder
> Pitched betwixt Heaven and Charing Cross.

The reference is to a Bible event, Jacob's dream at Bethel (Gen. 28:12).

9. *Others' use of Scripture.* Finally, be alert to ways in which the Bible is being used in public life today. Maintain a file of newspaper and magazine clippings; it will amaze you to discover the references to Scripture in the most unlikely sources. In due course a book will appear relating what contemporary people are saying about the Bible; you may edit that book. Meanwhile save every quotation, no matter how grotesque, if it comes from the lips of a prominent person.

Use the Bible often. It will do great things for your writing.

13

THE WRITER AS EDITOR

Sooner or later Christian writers seem to land—however briefly—in the editorial chair. They may launch their own paper; they may be hired by a publisher to edit a magazine; or they may be talked into cranking out a promotional bulletin for the local church. As soon as people discover that the writer has "a way with words," they will want him or her to do more than write.

For the blossoming author, a stint as editor of a paper can be valuable. If the experience forces one to write, teaches one to be flexible, gives one a variety of experiences and responsibilities, it can be a plus. If it kills the creative nerve and turns the writer into a drudge, a slave to the mimeograph or the printer, it is a waste.

Forty years ago the editor of a Christian magazine was usually a minister who spent his Sundays in the pulpit and weekdays at the editorial desk. His clothes were somber—blue suit and dark tie. He may not have known how to type, but his pencil was sharp, his prose was dignified and lucid, and his theology was well in hand.

Today's Christian magazine editor might be a young woman or a bearded young man fresh out of journalism school. He is able with a camera, competent in graphics, at home with communication skills. He might not be adept at hermeneutics, but he knows his Bible and he knows he is saved. He also knows how to bird-dog a story and make it lively reading. He buzzes around the world on jet aircraft, looking for copy. He is conversant in sports, music, and politics. In an interview he can switch quickly from soul talk to income-tax talk. And as for his dress . . . .

But today's editor is not tested by the standards of the past. (If he looks weird on television—so does everyone else!) The proof is the way he puts sentences together: either he is well trained or he is not. The finest training in the world is a chance to sit in the "slot," as we used to call it, and edit some kind of sheet, whether it be a church's monthly newsletter or an international magazine.

Leaving aside personal attributes, what qualities are desirable in an editor? I would list *clarity* as a top journalistic asset. To say exactly what we mean may not gain for us a Nobel Prize for literature, but it will fulfill the first test of effective communication. The editor's task is not only to write clearly, but also to see that those whose copy he or she edits express themselves intelligibly.

Today's editor must also be *brief.* Unless he learns to express himself tersely, no one will read him. Most editorials could be chopped in half with no great loss to the reading public.

The elimination of adjectives and adverbs is a first step toward brightening one's style. Tiresome clichés such as "for the most part," "on the other hand," and "as a matter of fact" should be rigorously blue-penciled. Many writers find it easier to be diffuse, but ours is a generation that likes brevity and clipped prose.

A *Rolling Stone* editor is quoted as saying he does not care whether what he prints is accurate or not. Christians have no option in the matter; their integrity is at stake. Facts must be documented and statements authenticated. A good editor spends much time writing letters asking for permission to quote. *Accuracy* means making an extra telephone call, checking the almanac, using standard reference works, making notes at the scene. The writer who relies solely on memory is unreliable, and the editor who prints that copy is irresponsible.

Balance is one of the editor's closest companions. The selection of stories, the arrangement on the page, the careful choice of words, all require care. Many evangelical editors have won the battle but lost the war because they failed to balance zeal with wisdom. An issue arises in the church and people speak out with some heat; what are editors to do? If prudent, one will weigh the facts and publish both sides. A careful reading of 1 Corinthians will give guidelines; the apostle Paul was a master of balance.

Christians frequently hold opposing views on contemporary issues. If we come out fighting in an editorial (unless we are fighting the devil), we may have to eat our words. That may be good for our humility, but it hurts the standing of our publication.

An editor with good balance will use journalistic *fairness.* It is not easy to state a case objectively when one's personal convictions are opposed to it, but readers are complimented when they are given a chance to decide an issue on the facts, fairly presented. A good test of an editorial would be whether a person opposed to the editor's position agrees that it is a fair statement.

Once I was asked to write a biographical sketch of a man I knew, a theologian with whose views of Scripture I totally disagreed. Eventually it was published in an evangelically oriented biographical dictionary. I told the truth, as fairly and objectively as I knew how. When I saw the theologian, he thanked me for the way I had treated him.

What should the editor write about? Here I may disagree with some, but I believe if an editorial does not take a stand on an important principle, it is no editorial. "The point of having an open mind, like an open mouth," wrote G. K. Chesterton, "is to close it on something solid." Even when the editor is required to deal with a subject that is not earth-shatteringly important, if one is wise he or she will look for the underlying principle and build a case on that. Then, several paragraphs down, bring in the current topic to illustrate the application of the principle.

Let's suppose a prominent person makes a racist remark. Or that vandals set fire to church headquarters. The editor can do one of several things:

- ignore the incident—which is a cop-out—and the paper runs the risk of being irrelevant.

- set one's sights on the person or persons involved. This is the argument *ad hominem*. An editor who deals in personalities may be bypassing the real issue, in which case one might better say nothing.

- mull over what was said or done, focusing on the event itself. This is the argument *ad hoc*.

- turn to the Bible and expound its truth and use the incident as a means of illustrating that truth. I call it the argument *ad veritatis*. It looks not only to the trees but to the forest; it penetrates to the heart of the issue and exposes the basic truth behind it.

Such an approach would keep the editor from trivializing editorials. The day will come when the Christian editor must really speak out as William Allen White did when he wrote his famous editorial, "What's the Matter with Kansas?" Then, because ammunition has not been wasted on small targets, the editor will be heard. Let the burning in one's soul be a divine discontent, not a hang-up. The minor irritations of life—such as potholes in the streets and congestion at the airport—are inconveniences of modern life. They can be presented legitimately in the public press through the letters column, or investigative or feature stories, or even through photographs. But not in editorials!

It is a sad commentary on Christian publications in North America that in the main they do not take clear editorial positions. Whatever the reason for this weakness, it is a glaring aberration. The Christian editor is a voice! He or she should speak out strongly and fearlessly, or fold up.

Every editor should keep his primary and secondary targets in mind as he writes. The primary target is the small portion of readers who will be in a position to do something about the matter. It could be an individual—the pastor of a church, or the governor of a state. It could be certain youth leaders, or union leaders, or business leaders, or denominational heads.

The secondary target is the readership whom the editor wants to inform about what he is writing to the primary target. That includes everyone who picks up the sheet and turns to the editorial page.

Suppose the editor is dealing with the question of prayer in the public schools. Regardless of the position he takes, he wants Congress to know how he (that is, his journal) feels. The senators and congressmen become his primary target, together with members of the Supreme Court. But he also wants his readers to know what he is saying to the heads of government so that he can build support for what he believes is a noble cause. The readers become the secondary target.

When the *New York Times* publishes an editorial about the presidency, it expects the clipping to show up on the desk in the Oval Office. Otherwise, why write it? But the secondary effects will also be great.

Earlier in this century Upton Sinclair wrote a bitter book about the press, calling it *The Brass Check*. The brass check was a token used in houses of prostitution. Sinclair's point was that the great newspapers of America had prostituted themselves for their owners, the money barons. Reporters and editors were "the kept press." And it was largely true; all the principal newspapers of America, with few exceptions, were rock-ribbed organs of conservatism.

Today everything has changed. Newspaper editors of America are no longer advocates of reactionary economics. Reporters no longer cower in fear of losing their jobs; they belong to the American Newspaper Guild. They have become bold and sophisticated—and skeptical. That is why we need men and women sitting in the editorial seat who have a Christian worldview and have learned not to mock. It is not that Christians are better journalists, or have more compassion, or can write better editorials on current issues, or believe more deeply in democracy. It is simply that we have hope in Christ.

In today's world, I believe, Christian editors can make outstanding contributions, no matter what publication they edit.

But they must beware of two diabolical temptations they will face every time they go to press. The first is to stoop to attack other Christians for what they have said or done. The other is to use their publication to promote a movement rather than for the glory of Jesus Christ.

Finally, let me tell you about four editors, of whom I knew two personally, while the others will perhaps remain forever unknown.

One was a student editor at the University of Michigan; today he is religion writer for a national news magazine. He is a Christian, and on the last day of his student editorship he devoted his entire editorial column to declaring his Christian faith.

The second was a student editor at Long Beach State University in California. He did not wait until his term of service was about up; he kept bringing Jesus Christ into his editorials, giving ringing endorsements to the various campus groups that were spreading Christianity. He was threatened; at times he had to be protected as he made his trips to the printer. But, for the most part, the student body liked the way he wrote and did not mind his religious orientation. His editorials made a hit.

The third was an editor of *Life* magazine back in the 1950s, when it was the most popular periodical in America. He wrote an Easter editorial in which he said:

> The resurrection is a vast watershed in history or it is nothing. It cannot be tested for truth; it is the test of lesser truths. No light can be thrown on it; its own light blinds the investigator. It does not compel belief; it resists it. But once accepted as fact, it tells more about the universe, about history, and about man's state and fate than all the mountains of other facts in the human accumulation.[6]

That editorial was no doubt quoted in pulpits all over the world during the Easter season of 1956. It was a fresh evaluation of an ancient truth; it challenged modern men and women to abdicate their contemporaneity and to see that truth is not something to be mined out of a quarry, but rather something to be distilled from God's action in history.

The fourth was an editorial writer for *Fortune* magazine, undoubtedly a layman as was the *Life* writer. In the January, 1940, issue of this sophisticated publication, the *Fortune* editor reflected that more than charts and graphs of business trends were needed to give significance to life. He spoke of churches that preached only relative and secondary values, thereby hastening the disintegrating, downward spiral of society. (He could have said the same for newspapers, including Christian journals.)

"There is only one way out of the spiral," he wrote, "and that way out is the sound of a voice, not our voice, but a voice coming from something beyond ourselves, in the existence of which we cannot disbelieve."

Today many people have stopped listening to that voice and have begun listening to other voices—voices of darkness from the occult. It is the responsibility of the Christian editor to remind the world—including the clergy—that there is a voice of truth out there; that the Spirit of God is speaking, and has spoken, and we had best hearken.

14

THE EXCITEMENT OF FICTION

Is there fire in your bones? Are you straining at the leash with something you feel God has given you to say? Are you ready to tackle the most exciting kind of writing there is? Will you pay the price and meet the standard? Then you can write fiction, and it will be published.

What a ridiculous statement! How can I make it? Easy. You see, it happened to me, and it may very well happen to you.

Several years ago I declared in print that I would never become a novelist. It is not the first time God has made me a liar. In 1986 Crossway Books published my novel, *The Doomsday Connection*, which is stark, unalloyed, unmitigated fiction. In the glow of that event I have no hesitation in saying to you, "Yes! Do it! Jump in, the water's fine."

My task in this chapter is not to make you more spiritual. Your spiritual state is between you and your Lord. My task now is to examine road blocks that are preventing you from being successful. And by successful I mean: your fiction meets the Christian standard, it is published, and it has a good reception by the reading public.

Our commitment as Christian writers is to present by every legitimate medium the gospel of Jesus Christ, that men and women might read, understand, become convinced, be saved, and enter the kingdom of God. To that end we seek to equip ourselves with skills and techniques; and one such skill is storytelling.

Some people question whether fiction is significant or important enough to be used in serving God's kingdom. I simply point to the impact that *Pilgrim's Progress* has made on human souls in the nearly four centuries since John Bunyan wrote it. Or I would refer the questioner to Jesus himself, whose appeal to his listeners was due in good measure to his charm as a storyteller. I could add a reference to more recent titles such as *Ben Hur, In His Steps, The Robe,* The Chronicles of Narnia, and others.

Take another tack. Think of the enormous influence of works of fiction on the opinions and customs of humankind. Magdeleine de Scudéry was a French novelist who prescribed the manners that were eventually adopted by English society. Let me add to her novels a few other works of fiction that formed public opinion and affected human behavior: *Don Quixote, A Tale of Two Cities, The Scarlet Letter, Madame Bovary, Ramona, Uncle Tom's Cabin, The Jungle, Lady Chatterley's Lover, Main Street, Elmer Gantry, Ulysses, Lolita.* Do I make my point? Fiction is dynamite!

Of all the forms of literature, fiction is the most fascinating, the most tantalizing, the most powerful, the most dangerous, the most exacting, the most frustrating—and, for the author, perhaps the most rewarding. Where a nonfiction book from a Christian writer can provide the reader with information and inspiration, a good short story or novel can do more. It can give positive enjoyment. It can cause people to read not because they ought to, but because they want to. Reading worthwhile fiction is one of the pleasures of life, and writing such fiction is a work that reflects the Creator's touch.

But writing *for the Lord* can only be a response to a higher call, for Christian writers are not satisfied simply to be published. They aim to present truth, and they know that fiction (whatever else it may be) can become a superb teaching tool. Ten words about eternal life, planted in a well-told story, will reach many who would not think of going to church or picking up a religious book. Alex Comfort has said that the novel is the foremost literary form for exerting pressure on the growth and forming of ideas. Kurt Vonnegut goes further and says that writers are the most important members of society.

Before moving into a discussion of the technical problems involved in fiction writing, I would like to clear the air by saying:

First, the popular interest in fiction is as enthusiastic as ever. Witness the preponderance of fictional episodes on television. People are always ready to be diverted by a good story. I say this despite the fact that 85% of books published in the United States are nonfiction.

Second, academic creative-writing courses, unless taught with consummate skill, will not produce a published novelist.

Third, Christian fiction is not necessarily "biblical" fiction.

Fourth, the purpose of Christian fiction is not to preach but to depict and describe, and to let readers draw their own conclusions.

Fifth, it is not necessary to make the reader wade through stagnant pools of floating garbage in order to reach a meaningful beachhead.

I do not claim to be a genius, a master, or an expert in this field. *The Doomsday Connection* is not the great American novel. Nevertheless I shall use it for illustrative purposes when it seems appropriate, because it overcame seemingly insurmountable obstacles. I learned how it is done professionally, and I dare to raise the question, "How does one write a novel, and how does one get it published?" Here is my answer.

Finding the basic premise

Without this foundation there is no story. The writer must begin by asking, What is my story about? In one sentence, what am I trying to say? The premise may not be clear at first; in my case, it took nearly two years before I was able to give my principal character a valid reason for his action that precipitated the story line—and then it came in a suggestion from a friend. Once that was settled, the premise was obvious. Everything that happened later was simply fallout: a series of conflicts and decisions forced on people by the main character's response to the basic premise.

R. V. Cassill says there are basically only two fiction stories: Cinderella, and Jack and the Beanstalk. In one the basic premise is that no matter how adverse the circumstances, virtue is rewarded. In the other, youth with ambition overcomes gigantic obstacles to achieve fame and success. Here are some other basic premises: honesty defeats duplicity, crime does not pay, egotism leads to loss of friends and failure, unbridled ambition is self-defeating, love conquers even over death.

In the case of my novel, the premise is that unless the heart is right, scientific brilliance leads to tragedy. In Dickens' *A Christmas Carol* the theme is, generosity is better than miserliness. In Dostoevsky's *The Brothers Karamazov*, Christ brings meaning into a meaningless world.

Establishing the setting

This could also include selecting the genre. Is the story to take place in the recent past, the distant past, or the present? Is it to have a rural or an urban cast? Will it deal with adventure, or is it about the interior lives of people? Will it concentrate on youth or age, on poor folk or wealth, on industry or indolence? Will the action of the novel be compressed within a brief time span, or is it to be spread over a long period? Will it be a story of personal growth or of deterioration, or both? Or is it sci fi or fantasy?

Rolvaag's *Giants in the Earth* and Dostoevsky's *Crime and Punishment* were stories of character growth. Fitzgerald's *Tender Is the Night* and O'Hara's *Appointment in Samarra* simply recorded a character's undoing. Setting is also affected by progression. Will the story unroll straightforwardly, as in Steinbeck's *Grapes of Wrath,* or will it be basically a flashback, as in Edith Wharton's *Ethan Frome,* or a series of flashbacks, as in Conrad's *Lord Jim* and Miller's drama, *Death of a Salesman?*

Fixing the problem

The basic premise must be portrayed as a problem if the story is to hold interest. In *A Christmas Carol* the problem was to loosen up Mr. Scrooge, the miser. In *The Brothers Karamazov* the premise is unfolded in a murder mystery: who killed the elder Karamazov? In my *The Doomsday Connection* the problem faced by the lead character was: if people realized that the world was actually coming to an end in two days, how would they react?

One difficulty in writing the novel is that its complete structure is almost never clear at the beginning. Many skilled writers have confessed that they do not know how the story they are currently writing will turn out, yet they keep to their schedule. You can now understand why novels often have to go through several drafts. The author has to discover the bone structure or framework within which the basic premise will work out its conclusion.

Researching the background

Research is what separates the amateurs from the professionals. The author must know the story's environment thoroughly, and it may take months and years to acquire that knowledge. Like everything else, research can be overdone, and so much time can be spent on it that the story never gets written. Usually, however, the author errs on the side of incompleteness.

Two of the finest novels of the nineteenth century, Tolstoy's *War and Peace* and Thackeray's *Henry Esmond*, were laid in the time of the Napoleonic wars, but were written half a century later. In each case the painstaking research produced literature that makes marvelous reading even today. In my novel I chose for a setting middle-class passengers traveling on a transcontinental airliner. Using a tape recorder, I interviewed pilots, copilots, flight engineers, flight attendants, weather experts, electronic experts, and investigated airplanes on my own; and that was only a part of the research the novel required.

Characterization

The secret of successful fiction lies not so much in intriguing plots or skill in dialog as in the development of characters. If the story's characters are well molded, authentic and human, and exhibit traits that interest the reader, the story will succeed. In preparation, the novelist needs to line out full-blown biographical sketches of the leading characters. One needs to live with them, sleep with them, and come to know them as members of the family.

Dorothy Sayers' most successful character was Lord Peter Wimsey, about whom she wrote several books. She knew him so well that she sketched a *Who's Who* account of him, listing his antecedents, his education, his war record, his clubs, his honors, and his politics. My critics insisted on calling some of my characters "mere sticks" until I set out to put flesh on their bones and make them come alive with full-blown backgrounds.

Some of the world's best stories, such as *Wuthering Heights*, have glaring technical weaknesses, but the personalities Emily Brontë describes are so vivid that the reader overlooks the faults. Many immortal tales include unnatural coincidences and natural disasters that are obviously contrived, but the author's magnificent characterizations carry the day.

We must never forget that while in real life people frequently act "out of character," in fiction they never do. Fictional characters can only be themselves, which is why authors frequently complain that once they have created their people, they are unable to control them.

It is well if the author maintains a certain detachment from the characters; they should not be simply facets of the author's own personality. Each should have independent integrity so that when they are thrown together they react on one another. That is what creates conflict, and conflict is the basis of plot. My despair of ever writing fiction was fostered by the feeling that I had no competence in creating plots. I have since been taught the truth: that *the basic premise forces a decision; the decision is made in the midst of conflict; the conflict reveals the character for what it truly is. The character's decision, or lack of it, propels the action, develops the story, thickens the plot, and moves it toward a climax through a series of complications.*

Perhaps now you are ready for a brief experiment. Take a sheet of paper and write the name of a fictional character you would like to use in a story. Write the full name, the age, sex, place of birth, names of parents, and the parents' vocations. Now tell us where this person grew up, what schools were attended, and for how long. Describe the person. How tall? Slim or stout? What color eyes and hair? Prominent characteristics? Shape of nose and chin? What kind of hands and voice?

Briefly note the person's outstanding tastes. What about friends? Social conditions and environment? Recreation if any? Vices? Church connections? Physical or mental illness? What does the person do for a living? None of this may appear in the story, but it will help you to become acquainted. You should be able to get inside this character's head and think as he or she thinks.

And now for the big one: what trait or quality in this person could possibly lead him or her into conflict?

Conflict

Without conflict there is no story. The more direct and pointed the conflict, the greater the complications; and the greater the complications, the more demand there is for further decisions to be made, which in turn increases the complications and heightens the conflict. Thus the interest of the readers is quickened; they "can't put the book down," they "have to see how it turns out." The book becomes what is known in the trade as a "page turner." It is exciting.

Here are some common elements of conflict: A teenager is fed up with parental restrictions. A woman rebels against masculine arrogance. A soldier is taken prisoner. Two women quarrel over a man. A sensitive personality struggles with guilt or is warped by a desire for revenge. A human being is caught up in a struggle against the forces of nature. An unbeliever is driven by circumstances to faith. A bitter person is confronted by indomitable love.

Several conflicts appear in my novel. A powerful woman is determined to get even with her brother. A prostitute tries to break her drug habit and shed her past. A secretary battles her own conscience. A minister is confronted by his mother, his church, and his God. In each case the conflict reveals the character for what it really is.

Resolution

A sense of dramatic fulfillment is the mark of true literature. That does not mean all loose ends have to be tied up. Henry James' *Portrait of a Lady* ends with the bare possibility of a satisfying encounter. Herman Wouk's *Caine Mutiny* leaves the young man with nothing but a good feeling of hope. The novelist lets the reader take the story in his imagination to a conclusion that seems implied.

Some avant-garde novelists make sport of this whole method of writing fiction; to them plots are unnecessary, because nothing is ever resolved. Fortunately only a fraction of the reading public is interested in their material. Unless some resolution is provided for a story, most readers will be disappointed and will be quick to say so.

How did these principles work out in the construction of *The Doomsday Connection?* I have indicated that the environment was the 1980s and the characters were middle-class Americans. The story's basic premise derived from a conviction in the mind of a young computer genius that Christians don't really believe that the Lord Jesus is coming back and are not ready for him. The resulting problem stemmed from the boy's attempt to prove his premise.

After the novel's first "final" draft was rejected—by a reader, two publishers, and two East Coast literary agents—there followed a time of agonizing reappraisal. The major flaw in the story was its lack of clear resolution. There was no climax, only a dangling ending. As one critic wrote, "You promised the end of the world, but you didn't deliver it." Some of the characters were indifferently drawn, and conflict was skimped. To embellish the description of characters was not difficult. To add conflict, I provided uproar in a church, a gun chase, a raid on a Christian television station, and two dead bodies. As for the conclusion, it came to me quietly one day in my study in a passage of the Old Testament. I immediately telephoned my publisher, shared it with him, and he agreed and told me to go ahead. The rest was simply implementation.

In their book *The Enjoyment of Literature,* Boas and Smith name three standards by which to measure good fiction: artistry, vitality, and significance. I can think of no better goals for a person who would write literature. But in the pits where copy is ground out, I find three other requirements to be equally essential: research, critiquing, and rewriting.

Research

The main purpose of research is to provide accurate material. The writer should work from both a notebook and a cassette recorder. The writer should be thorough, observing not only ideas, phrases, and emphases, but also body language and particular gestures. Tom Wolfe says of research, "It's hard, it's embarrassing, it's time-consuming," but it pays off. Wolfe adds, "Don't underestimate the evocative and symbolic properties of circumstantial detail."

Critiquing

My novel could not have been written without extensive help from other people. Friends spent many hours with me in critique groups, analyzing characters, improving phrasing, and suggesting scenes of confrontation. I recall one friend saying, "I want to see someone die in this story, perhaps two people." Much to my surprise, two ultimately did. Another friend said of a man and a prostitute, "Have him rip her dress." The thought had never occurred to me, but it worked. Still others unlocked story-line problems that had baffled both me and my editor friends.

So even though I had recognizable limitations as a novelist, notably in the area of plot construction, others managed to bail me out. Exposing one's writing to the criticism of others—even friendly criticism—is not the most joyous of occupations, and I would not urge it if I did not know from experience that it yields results. The vast majority of the suggestions I received had merit, and many comments were extremely valuable and even indispensable. To solo writers who feel no need of such help, but are still unpublished, I say, "Try this route. Leave your ego at home, and go for it. You are bound to improve your material." As with all criticism, you can take it or leave it. Usually I take it, gratefully. Ultimately, of course, there comes a time when the manuscript is back in your lap. All human help must be foregone so that God can take over. When that happens, the story and the storyteller are one.

Rewriting

After others have made hentracks over one's copy, it seems a hopeless task to go back to the wearisome thing and do it over. When I asked earlier, "Will you pay the price?"—this is the price! It is exactly this discipline that will turn out the finished product. Fiction writers should remember that they are writing for the market—which is what academic courses in creative writing tend to ignore. What a terrible waste of time and energy it is to keep polishing a story when the market for such material is weak and the editors are totally uninterested in it! Find out first what the fiction editors want and what they don't want. Then you can think about a book.

Our century has not been without good Christian fiction,

even though the yield has not been as fruitful as one would wish. Short stories are not as much in demand as they were a few decades ago, but other forms of fiction are as popular as ever. Novels by Helen Waddell, C. S. Lewis, Charles Williams, Eugenia Price, Elisabeth Elliot, Catherine Marshall, Frederick Buechner, Madeleine L'Engle, Calvin Miller, and others have been justly acclaimed. Their success speaks for itself. But it is worth noting that the novels of Jane Austen, George MacDonald, Anthony Trollope, and other church-related 19th-century writers are still being reprinted. The demand for good fiction remains unfulfilled; and meanwhile films and television are waiting in the wings. What is holding us back?

One of the most stunning acts of recent history was the visit President Anwar Sadat of Egypt paid to Israel in 1972. He launched a peace process between two nations that had been enemies for 3000 years. Why did he do it? He gave his reasons, and others have speculated. One possible clue lies in two novels by an American Christian minister, *The Magnificent Obsession* and *The Robe*. Someone who knew Sadat well reports that as a young man languishing in a British prison for his political activity in Egypt, Sadat read those books, and that they deeply impressed him.

Should you write fiction? Ask your heavenly Father. Remember that the common people heard Jesus of Nazareth gladly, and when they gathered around him, he told them stories. The preaching of the gospel is a magnificent calling, and I love to hear a fine sermon. But had I been sitting on a window ledge in Troas 1900 years ago, listening to the apostle Paul preach till midnight, I might, like young Eutychus in the book of Acts, have gone to sleep and toppled to the ground. On the other hand, had I been in Galilee by the lakeside, listening to the Master, I would have been bright-eyed and bushy-tailed when he began with the words, "The kingdom of heaven is like a man from a far country . . . ."

15

GO AFTER THE INTERVIEW

Do you want zest? A fresh breeze blowing through your life? Get an interview. Do you want fun? Get an interview. Do you want to write something that will glorify Jesus Christ? Find the Christian you most admire and get an interview.

Interviewing is live action. To ask questions, to record answers, is to create a happening.

As a junior editor at the University of California, I followed a hunch, drove to Stanford University, and interviewed the student who recently had stolen the famous Stanford Axe from his hated rivals at Cal. (Of course, the hated rivals had stolen it from Stanford in the first place.) That one interview nearly catapulted me into the editorship of the *Daily Californian*, even though I was lamentably unqualified.

A young woman asked Paul Little for an interview at the Decision School of Christian Writing. Little was a prime architect of the 1974 Lausanne Congress on world evangelization in Switzerland. She got the interview, and two weeks later Paul Little was killed in a highway accident. His farewell message of faith became Joyce Ellis's breakthrough into national print.

Most people—even busy and important people—like to be interviewed. Christians are happy for an opportunity to speak of their faith in Jesus Christ. Unless considerable skill is exercised, however, the results of an interview can be disappointing.

What are the pitfalls to avoid in obtaining and writing a successful interview?

1. *A poor subject.* Many hours can be wasted in interviewing someone unworthy of our time. For the Christian writer an interview is a means of spreading the gospel by revealing Jesus Christ as real and contemporary in someone's life. To ask a subject about this faith in Christ when the subject has never been known to mention it is to take a risk. Bad trees do not produce good fruit, and if the point of an interview is to explore the spiritual aspect of an unspiritual subject's life, it will fail. On the other hand, the late Dag Hammarskjöld was a person of deep faith, but no reporter ever asked him about it. A great story was missed.

2. *Inane questions.* The number one rule to remember in interviewing is that *the questions are more important than the answers.* By asking perceptive questions, sharply and directly, without softening or qualifying them, the interviewer may evoke replies that will make an excellent story. But what kind of questions? The answer is, the kind of questions readers of the article would ask if they had the opportunity—the questions that are on people's minds, that bring out the real personality, that reveal not just a public figure but a human being,

that dig into sources and processes. To ask only the same questions others have asked is to end with a dull story.

The best interviews are those in which the questions are thought out in advance and jotted down. It will require time and thought, but the effort pays off. Often in the give and take of interviews the conversation will veer into unprofitable channels; having written questions will bring it back on track. Written questions will not be the only questions, but they will keep the dialog from wilting.

Interviewers sometimes use traps to elicit dramatic statements from their subjects. A reporter once asked President Truman if he thought the Alger Hiss case was a "red herring" drawn across the path of Congress to keep it from considering important legislation. Truman said, "Yes." The reporter's paper headlined, "Truman calls Hiss case a red herring." The "statement" received enormous publicity and became an election issue. But Truman stated later that he never said it.

Christian interviewers do not need to use traps or devices. They are not interested in sensationalism, but in the truth, and in asking questions they remain sensitive and polite.

Interviewing includes many things, but basically it is the art of getting inside a human soul, discerning the springs of motivation, what priorities the person has set, what were the reasons for doing certain things in the past, and why the particular course was chosen for the future.

The Christian interviewer's task is not quite the same as the secular journalist's, either in style or content. Crude and hurtful questions are avoided. There are non-Christian gentlemen and gentlewomen in the business of interviewing and it behooves Christians to be no less gracious. Arrogant and impudent questions may create headlines, but, like inane and irrelevant questions, they do nothing for the cause of Jesus Christ.

3. Faulty equipment. A tape recorder that fails to record is worse than no tape recorder. Twice I have had to contend with equipment breakdowns in the midst of important interviews. The writer must be prepared—and should carry a pencil.

4. Deficient writing. It is frustrating to read an interview with an interesting person and find the ideas are poorly expressed, the questions are obvious, the replies are banal, and no effort has been made to delete the irrelevancies. To translate the hesitant spoken word into crisp written prose is part of the writer's vocation. When the writer fails, the interview comes apart.

The interview need not be written in question-and-answer style; that could prove a handicap if the story is for a newspaper. A journalistic interview strives to capture atmosphere and background as well as comments, and pictures usually accompany the story. If the interview is for a magazine, however, and carries more than local significance, the reader will appreciate having before him the actual words of the person interviewed, statement by statement.

5. Dull layout. We found at *Decision* magazine that to arrange questions and answers under "Q." and "A." was to kill interest. For example, let us suppose the subject of the interview is a church leader from Hong Kong. The layout could present the material this way:

Q. Do you think the church will survive the present Communist opposition in China?

A. Probably. I have faith.

Q. Do you think there will be a revival in China?

A. Well, you know, it's always possible to have a revival anywhere. God is still sovereign, and there are various elements involved in revival that are present in every church situation, either actively or in latent form.

A better journalistic arrangement would be:

Do you think the church in China will survive? I have faith.

What are the prospects of revival? The elements involved in revival are always present in the church. God is still sovereign.

One of the finest exercises for a budding writer is to seek out important people who come to town and ask them for interviews. It helps if the writer has made an arrangement first with some publication; that gives a certain credential. But the credential is not really necessary—after all, you can always say you are gathering material for a book!

Sometimes after conducting an interview I have gone over the material and realized I forgot to ask the most important question. It happened when I interviewed former President Eisenhower: I discovered to my chagrin that I had failed to ask him what he thought of Jesus Christ. I was able to get his answer by way of his secretary, but it was careless journalism.

A year or two later when interviewing Captain Eddie Rickenbacker, I determined not to make the same mistake. I put it to him bluntly: "Captain Eddie, what does Christ mean to you?"

"What do you mean, what does Christ mean to me?" he roared. "Why, he means everything to me!"

Having sat in dozens of press conferences with Billy Graham, I have been fascinated by the ease with which he fields questions. Yet I must say the questions put to him by the reporters are often routine and deal with trivial matters. Such stories make poor reading. To toss three or four questions at a subject and consider him "interviewed" is ridiculous.

Once at a press conference in Copenhagen a Danish reporter asked Mr. Graham, "What's so special about you?"

"There's nothing special about me," was the reply. It was an object lesson in how not to conduct an interview.

I do not wish to imply that questions should always be gentle. Once in the early 1960s when Mr. Graham was in an airport, about to leave for an evangelistic crusade in Alabama, a reporter asked him, "Will you permit blacks to counsel whites who come forward at your rallies?"

The question was loaded, for in a hundred years of evangelism in the South, no such mixing was permitted; to suggest that a black Christian could lead a white non-Christian to Jesus was unthinkable—and not just in the South.

Mr. Graham's reply was, "Our counselors will conduct themselves in the same way they do at all our crusades."

It sounded mild, but it meant the end of segregated evangelism. It was a historic interview.

The best interviews, of course, are privately arranged, with an hour or an hour and a half of time provided. In that period the questioner can probe the background effectively. When I spent an hour with pianist Van Cliburn, we went back to his Baptist childhood in Texas. With former senator Harold Hughes it meant reviewing his early days as a trucker in Iowa. With Kimo, the Auca killer who became a Christian, we began in the jungles of Ecuador.

Begin at the beginning! Then let the questions lead gradually to the adolescent period, where a good deal of time should be spent. Adolescence is not only a time of growing up, it is a time of decision making. Was there a Christian decision, a commitment to Jesus Christ in the story? No matter what the later accomplishments of the interviewee, this is the heart of the matter. It is of supreme importance that all the factors in that commitment surface.

If the subject says, "I made my decision for Christ when I was 17," that is not good enough. How did it come about?

What other people were involved? What were the precipitating elements? What was the subject's state of mind? What actually did the person do or say? How was the church affected? What happened immediately after the decision?

Here is the way Augustine described how he felt and acted during the period when he was making up his mind about Jesus Christ: "In the emotional excitement created by my hesitation, I engaged in various random actions. I tugged at my hair and pounded my forehead and locked my fingers and hugged my knees. . . . My introspection plumbed the secret depths and brought together all my misery in plain sight of my heart, so that a great storm broke, bringing a shower of tears."

And this was written 14 years after the event!

The only way to secure such details is to probe with persistent questions. Sometimes the interviewees will be cooperative; if they are not, of course, nothing is gained by antagonizing them.

Print is a powerful medium. It is doubtful that Augustine would be able to publish his famous *Confessions* on today's market without running the risk of libel. For the interviewer, obtaining permission to print is all-important. Once the story is written, it is mandatory that a copy be sent to the subject for approval and consent in writing. Permission must be granted! To have the subject come forth with a statement afterward that he was "misquoted" does nothing for the interviewer's reputation. If the writer has the green light, it is "all systems go," but not until then.

Among the gracious people I have interviewed I remember particularly Secretary of the Navy Claude M. Swanson, who received me aboard the *U.S.S. Indianapolis* at anchor in Hilo Bay, Hawaii. I also fondly remember Irving Berlin, the song writer, whom I escorted about the city of Juneau, Alaska, back in 1938, and Senator Mark Hatfield, whom I interviewed for *Decision* when he was governor of Oregon.

Secretary of the Interior Harold Ickes, the "curmudgeon," refused to talk with me, but I interviewed his wife. J. Edgar Hoover also refused to allow me to interview him, but offered to answer any written questions. I submitted the questions, and one day I was informed that the FBI was at our reception desk waiting to see me. The agent in charge had the replies to my questions.

As a young sports reporter, I was ordered by the city editor of a San Francisco newspaper to interview "Navy Bill" Ingram, a football coach, and ask him when he intended to resign (he had just lost a football game 20-0 a few minutes earlier). I wish I could live that experience again; I would tell the city editor what I thought of his suggestion.

At *Decision* magazine it became my practice to interview veteran warriors of the Christian faith. Knowing they would not be around forever, I sought, as it were, a legacy to leave to our readers. In that spirit I interviewed Ethel Waters, L. Nelson Bell, Wilbur M. Smith, Clyde W. Taylor, A. Lindsey Glegg, Vance Havner, Corrie ten Boom, Harry Denman, C. E. Autrey, and others. Many veteran warriors are now gone, but others are still with us, waiting for some aspiring writer to call on them.

I am acquainted with at least three women writers who first selected a theme, then taped interviews with several prominent Christian women, and had them published in paperback. Publishers are name conscious; if the author's name fails to move them, sometimes the name of the subject will. Once a writer gets into the habit of interviewing people, a book may well result.

Some of the finest interviews, I have learned, may not come from prominent people at all, but from little people who have lived greatly with God. This is mother-lode country. If you can find a high-schooler, a young adult, a housewife, a missionary, a teacher, a scientist, a bus driver, a personnel worker, an itinerant evangelist with a beautiful testimony, it will carry an appeal far beyond the ordinary religious story.

A little elderly woman named Pearl Goode used to travel the Billy Graham circuit with the team. She never associated with the team however; she stayed in small hotels and spent all her time praying. Often she did not even appear at the crusade meetings. Her story appeared in *Decision* under the title, "There Is Nothing Like It."

If you can remember the simple ground rules for interviewing, if you will make yourself into a window through which your readers can see spiritual reality, you will be published—never fear. The stories are there; all you need to do is go after them.

16

THE CRITIQUE GROUP

It happens all the time to writers: we come to a place where we don't know what to do with the pages we've been working on. The piece simply isn't turning out right. We think we see what is wrong, but we don't know how to fix it. Or, the editor has sent it back without giving any reasons for rejecting, and we have reached a point where we are ready to give up. We need help. To whom shall we turn? To God, certainly. But beyond that—

Let me present some options for the writer who is looking for some help in this situation:

1. The professional house. Certain companies advertise nationally, offering to give your manuscript a thorough critique. The advertisement carries the names of several famous writers. No doubt they are honest, and no doubt they will do a workmanlike job. But they are expensive.

2. The individual expert. This person may be a literary agent, a retired editor, or a free-lance writer who, among other things, works on people's manuscripts for a fee. Such a person is usually competent, and may also prove congenial and sympathetic. The writer will have to decide whether such help is worth the cost.

3. *The visiting editor.* This person is one you can meet at a writers' conference. The editor will be glad to talk with you during consultation time, and charge nothing. Such a contact is certainly valuable, and you will learn whether there is market interest in your writing; but detailed help is of course impossible in such a setting, because the interviews last only 15 or 20 minutes.

4. *The critique group.* There is no better way for a beginner to be initiated into the writing profession than by joining a critique group, particularly if it is broadly Christian in its orientation. Critique groups make an admirable expression of Christianity because they allow people to help each other, and thus become the functioning body of Christ. Usually the groups have no qualifying restrictions. They require no fee beyond bringing refreshments occasionally. By their very nature they introduce newcomers into the fellowship of Christian writers, and a person soon learns the intricacies, the vocabulary, and the people and institutions involved in spreading the gospel through the published word. From the group one learns not what to write, but how to present it.

All over the United States, and in many other parts of the English-speaking world, Christian writers are discovering that it is hard to be objective about one's own output. They are forming house groups for mutual help, and are finding that encouragement is the greatest stimulus to writing. Some of the groups are more successful than others; in fact, many groups fade out after a few attempts at meeting, for lack of good leadership. But the principle behind the critique group is sound: writers need other writers. And the record shows that many successful writers today credit the support of a critique group with giving them their professional start.

My first introduction to such a group occurred during the early 1960s. I was invited to meet with some writers in St. Paul, Minnesota, and for ten years we gathered monthly on Saturday afternoons at the home of a Christian author. Someone has calculated that during those years, 28 books were published by its members. For the past eight years a similar group has been meeting in a home in La Mesa, California, and is producing articles, songs, and books. Two of its members have become editors. Similar successes can be gleaned from nearly every section of the United States and Canada.

What is a critique group and how does it function? Many seminars have been taught on the subject in writers' conferences, and many articles have appeared in print. I will limit myself to my own experience, but hasten to say that God is a God of infinite variety, and many different approaches can be made to this subject. What is presented here is drawn from personal observation of many groups; but whatever works, and brings results in print, has my full approbation, even though it be an entirely different approach from the one with which I am familiar. To deal with the simple logistics, I will use a question-answer form.

How large is the group? For best results it should include no fewer than three and no more than ten persons.

How much time does each person have? On the average, half an hour. To go beyond that is to deprive someone else of a turn. A short piece, such as a poem, may require less time.

Where do you meet? Usually in a private home, but any convenient place will do.

What time of day do you meet? Whenever people agree they should meet—morning, afternoon, or evening.

Do you serve refreshments? Coffee, fruit, or doughnuts are often provided. People take turns bringing them. It seems to work best if the writers do not interrupt the critiquing to indulge, but simply help themselves as they feel inclined.

What is the procedure? The writers sit in a comfortable circle and take turns, going around the room, each taking a half hour.

If the writer reads for half an hour, when is the critiquing done? The writer usually reads for only 10 or 15 minutes. The remainder of the half hour is used in critiquing what has been read.

How is that done? While the writer is reading, the critiquers are making notes on their pads. These notes can deal with general questions, or with specifics such as grammar, wording, points of fact or doctrine. After the reader finishes, the others go around the circle, offering their comments. The reader makes notes on the comments, and later may rewrite the piece to incorporate the suggested improvements.

It sounds pretty harsh, taking all that criticism. The critiquers are Christians. They are not there to criticize but to help. They are quite aware that the other writers are as sensitive as they are themselves.

Isn't there a temptation to argue and fight back? No. The rules require that the person reading is to remain silent and make notes while the critiquing is going on. If someone asks a question, the reader can reply but should not rebut, object, defend, or in any way interrupt the one offering a critique.

Isn't it true that some people can't take criticism? No one likes to have his work dissected and held up to the glare of contrary opinion. But the Christians in the critique group are careful to be gentle and to emphasize the good points in the writing, no matter how few. They do not wish to hurt. They are simply offering their opinion as to how the work can be improved. Once people realize that the critiquing provides really wonderful help, they learn to beg for it.

Suppose the writer doesn't agree with the critiques? There is nothing that says the writer has to follow the opinions of others. But many times those opinions touch on the very points of weakness in the writing.

Do they do anything else besides telling the writer what is wrong with the material? They certainly do. Experienced critiquers are always searching for a market for what they have just heard. They will make positive recommendations, mentioning contacts, outlets, and publishers who would be interested in the manuscript.

Does the reader pass around copies of what he or she is reading? Yes, that is a great help and speeds up the critiquing. But not everyone is able to do this.

Suppose the critique group completely misunderstands the meaning that the writer intended. Can't the others be set straight? Of course if one feels strongly about it, the group will gladly give up a few minutes at the end of the critiquing of the work so the writer can state what was meant. But the obvious response to that is, why didn't you say that in the first place?

Do you have any other rules and regulations? We try to have as few rules as possible. We do open with prayer. And if the group grows too large, we simply divide and form two groups.

Suppose someone reads something that isn't particularly religious? Our aim is to help people get into print, not to tell them what they should write. One of our members writes singing commercials for a chain of barber shops. Writers have many ways to witness for Christ besides writing.

Many other questions might be raised about the conduct of a critique group, and because we are all different, our groups are certain to be different. What works beautifully in Oregon may fizzle in Iowa. But one rule will apply in most situations: it is well to have at least one experienced, published writer in each group, if possible. Someone needs to take responsibility to see that the critiquing flows smoothly and easily. There is always the danger of one person "taking over," and without wise leadership, the group may end up simply pooling its ignorance.

Attendance each month will vary. People move, and groups change their character. But I can think of two reasons why the critiquers will keep coming month after month and year after year. One is a consistent, regular meeting time. The other is results. When writers begin to sell, other writers catch the spirit and come alive. The awarding of a contract to one member is a cause for celebration. Everyone rejoices, because everyone had a part in it. I can wish nothing better for you as a writer than participation in a lively, congenial, exciting, successful, producing critique group. It is sure to do things for your writing career.

17

THE BRIGHT SIDE OF REJECTIONS

If there is one person in the world with whom I empathize today, it is the lonely, isolated author who wants to write, has a story to share, believes in his qualifications, works hard, and gets nowhere. I know all about it, and, believe me, it doesn't have to be that way.

Early in this century young Jack London wrote *The Call of the Wild*, stuffed it in an envelope, and mailed it to the *Saturday Evening Post*. In the return mail he received a check for one thousand dollars. What's wrong with that story is that we cannot relate to it. Jack London was a genius. We are mere mortals of terrestrial design and orbit, but that doesn't mean we have to be ignorant. We can study the market and learn where to send material with a good chance of having it accepted. It's dandy to concentrate on self-expression, but it's quicker to send something to an editor who wants it.

If you wish to be published in a magazine, study several back issues carefully. See what the editor is attempting to do. By all means, make contact with the editor, if possible: take her to lunch, talk to her about her goals and purposes. If she wants to talk about your article, mention your research. Discuss photographs. If the editor happens to be male—what of it? Lunch is lunch, and you are a pro.

Ruth McKinney has kindly permitted me to reproduce her suggestions to aspiring writers wishing to submit something for publication.[7] She writes:

> After deciding on a market for your writing you are ready to prepare it for mailing to an editor. Manuscripts are judged by appearance as well as content, so you need to send out neat script. Before typing the final draft, a good craftsman checks his writer's tool kit:
> - Black typewriter or word processor ribbon, new.
> - White 8½" x 11" good quality bond paper.
> - Clean keys.
>
> Address the editor by name and title. This information is available in the current *Writers Market* or *The Religious Writer's Marketplace*.
>
> The senior editor of a large publishing house says that when his office receives a manuscript with words misspelled, corrections penciled in, and with the typing so dim it is hard to read, there is little chance of that manuscript being considered for publication.
>
> The editor wants copy that is in shape when it arrives at his desk. How can we get our writing into its best form? It will help to follow these basic steps for the final copy:
> - On page one type your name and address in the upper left-hand corner. The number of words should appear in the upper right-hand corner.
> - Begin the article about one-third of the way down the first page. Center your title and byline. Indent paragraphs five

spaces. Double space your copy and type on only one side of the paper.
- On each additional page, type your last name and the title of the article in the top left-hand corner. The page number goes at the top right-hand corner or in the center of the page.
- Leave a margin of about two inches on the left-hand side of the page, one inch at the top and bottom and on the right side.
- All quotations from letters and books when used in the body of your article would also be double spaced and given an extra indentation of five spaces to make them stand out.
- The submitting of poetry is similar to that of the article. Type your poem, double-spaced, on an 8½" x 11" sheet of paper, using one side of the paper only and keeping one poem to a page. If the poem is lengthy, number the consecutive pages and carry your name in the top left-hand corner on each page.

To make your task of mailing easier, here are a few suggestions:
- Make sure you are sending your manuscript to the right person.
- A small postage scale is inexpensive and worth the investment.
- Short stories and articles may be folded and mailed, provided they are less than six pages. Fold them into thirds. Longer articles and pictures are mailed flat with a cardboard backing. Always enclose a self-addressed stamped envelope with the same amount of postage on it as it takes to send the manuscript.
- Book manuscripts must be mailed flat. Use a book envelope or the box the typing paper came in. Send the pages loose without stapling. Clip sufficient postage to the first page of your manuscript.
- Pictures are identified on a separate sheet of paper. Do not mark on the backs of photographs.
- As many as seven poems may be folded and enclosed in an envelope for mailing.
- Keep a copy of all the manuscripts you send out. On the copy make a record of where you sent it and the date sent. If it is

returned, make a note of that date. Keep the record in a folder, under the title of the piece, alphabetically, in a steel cabinet, or on a computer disk.

Now let's assume that you have done everything by the book, and have even added a few prayers as you sent off your manuscript; but in spite of all your pains and hopes, it came back with a regretful note of rejection printed on pink paper. What to do? Give up? Many do. But there is an alternative. You can make adversity work for you. The name of the game is recycling. Here is how it works.

1. Make sure the manuscript is not still in the hands of an editor before you begin recycling. The obvious reason for that is that you may be embarrassed by selling the article twice. That has happened to people I know. They have sent the same article to two different publishers, have been accepted by both, and then have had to write one and say, "I'm sorry, you can't have it." This serves to blacklist the author in the eyes of the publisher. The writer won't sell anything there again. (The question of simultaneous submissions is discussed further at the end of this chapter.)

2. Find out from the editor exactly why it was rejected. Perhaps there is something seriously wrong with the manuscript. If there is something wrong, I urge you to move heaven and earth to locate it. (But remember—just as you need quiet in which to write, your editor needs relief from the phone ringing all day in order to edit.)

Editors can help you, if they have the time and interest. However, they have to be convinced that you don't have feelings of pride that will get in the way of your absorbing professional opinion regarding your product. If they think you will be embarrassed or miffed or put off by what they say, they won't say anything. Or, they'll say something bland like the wording of a rejection slip. If they really think you want to know, and you won't take offense, they will tell you what you want to know. They will be glad to, because they want to help you and encourage you.

Remember that one of the hardest lessons any professional has to learn is to beg for criticism. Compliments are nice, but they're not going to improve your copy. If you can adopt an attitude of openness toward everyone, from the neighbor boy to the editor-in-chief, regarding your cherished piece, you're going to be a writer.

3. Just rewrite it. Perhaps all this reject needed was a little more work and a little more polish. You sent it off before it was ready. Well, slip a piece of paper in the typewriter and try again. I remember a minister saying once that he had often left a home without praying and later regretted it, but he had never left a home after praying and later regretted it. I can say that I have never rewritten an article and regretted it. I always was able to improve it, even if it was just the punctuation, by running it through just once more.

If there is any doubt in your mind, take that nice clean manuscript that's come back with a rejection slip attached, sit down in your easy chair, and with your pencil in hand start to go through it. Read it again, and then you'll say, "Well, I see that could have been changed—too many adjectives in that sentence"—or whatever it is. Then by the time you've read it again, you've got it penciled. Now it's time for retyping. I think that many of our manuscript problems could be taken care of by just a little rewriting.

4. Salvage the best feature of the piece. Work it up by itself. Out of a long epic poem, a few lines may be really good. Well,

let's go with those lines and not worry about the epic. Here are four lines that I salvaged out of a poem by a woman from Sidney, New York. In the midst of all the rest of it, she had written this:

> Crumbled desires
> crushed pride
> bruised heart
> salvage for God.

As an editor I liked that because it has the idea that God can take the broken pieces of life and put them back together and make something out of us. In other words, the poem has hope in it. So, I decided to use those lines, even though the whole poem wasn't suitable.

Salvaging also works with articles. Sometimes you may have a good anecdote—work with it. It's like the oyster and the pearl. You build on it and wrap things around it, and pretty soon you've got an article. You send it in—and it's rejected! The editor might even say, "You had a good idea there." Well, the idea was the anecdote, and that was really the best thing about the piece. Why not salvage the anecdote? Why not lift that out and send that in? Every magazine has corners and little holes, because editors are conscious of the fact that solid type on a page has low readability. If they can break up the page with art work, white space, large type, or a poem, that will make people more interested in reading the message on that page. So I say, take the best feature of the article that has been rejected and work it up by itself.

What is the best feature? You can ask your friends again, and they will quickly pinpoint it for you. It will be that which is most interesting to the average reader.

5. Try casting the piece in a totally different form. If it was a devotional, try working it up as a dialog, or make it a children's story, or a play. Add to it, or shorten it, or do something different with it.

Maybe that's not what it needs. If a number of people have taken a poor view of the piece, that's a pretty good indication that something has to be changed. It needs to be attacked from a different point of view. That leads me to the sixth point.

6. Forget the piece of writing you have done which has been rejected, but use the idea behind it as a stimulant to a fresh piece.

Writing from a completely different angle—perhaps moving it from third person to first person—or vice versa—will often help. The original thought that you had was sound, you understand, but it needed a different kind of execution.

7. Send it out again, but make sure you don't send it back to the same editor. I don't need to tell you that many, many books have been sent out again and again and have been rejected; but when at last they have been accepted after the thirty-second turndown, they have turned out to be literary events. Publishers admit freely that they make mistakes in judging manuscripts.

Keep sending it out. If you believe in the manuscript and your friends believe in it, and they're not just trying to coddle you or make you feel good, go ahead. Send it out again, and perhaps from different editors you'll get ideas as to how to improve it, even if they don't accept it.

8. Read the manuscript to your critique group, with the comments of the editor who rejected it. Don't ask for sympathy, and don't try to justify yourself or argue why you think it's good.

You believe deep in your heart that your critics are wrong. Well, sometimes they are, of course. And we must never pay so much attention to our critics that we get discouraged or lose our creative edge. But, on the other hand, they are trying to help us. If they shoot holes in our boat, they'll hand us a bailing bucket. Remember that you are a pro, and pros don't cry. When you get these people to express themselves, write down their comments. Then you go back and you tackle the rewriting.

9. Don't pass up an opportunity to get your reject into print. If you are rejected by Editor A, you may hear about Editor B who may want material like yours. In your discussions with other writers, this kind of news is always bubbling to the surface. Don't pass up the chance to dig out what you have. Dust it off and send it in.

If your published writings are to be collected in a paperback, why not sneak that reject in with the others? It was just as good as your other writing, you believe. It just might make it, and then you will have it recycled.

10. Don't worry about what's in your file. A quarterback completes only a certain percentage of his passes. All of the great writers left behind cartons of unpublished manuscripts—Lewis, Wolfe, Hemingway, Kafka. Once in a while a publisher will release an "early book of Joyce Cary" or someone else, and it really doesn't have it. The author knew it—which is why he kept it in a carton. Don't be obsessed to see everything you've written in print. The past is prolog. What's in your file is preparation for the good things you have yet to write. Samuel Johnson is recorded as saying, "No man but a blockhead ever wrote, except for money." That, from a Christian perspective, is pure tommyrot. But there is the other extreme of the ivory tower. Write to be published, and you will be published.

11. Remember that your best writing is always yet to come. While endeavoring to recycle your old stuff, be sure that you are engaged in something new and fresh. Keep on the lookout for new ideas. The experience that you have tomorrow may be the catalyst that will get you into print in a wonderful way. God's mercies are new every morning, and so are our writing opportunities.

Before we leave the subject of recycling, something must be said about the manuscript that has already been accepted and is in print. Many authors simply cut out the article, cover it with a query letter, and send it to another editor. Something that appeared in a Baptist publication can be sold to the Lutherans. Professional writers sometimes sell their articles 20 or 30 times over. In this way they keep dozens, even hundreds, of manuscripts circulating all the time.

Other ways of recycling have proved equally successful. Simultaneous submissions are now accepted by many magazine and book houses—but the author should always notify each editor that it is, in fact, a simultaneous submission.

Perhaps you write a newspaper column. After so many columns have appeared, the newspaper itself might be talked into publishing a selection in book form.

Devotional articles appearing in magazines can be collected and reprinted in booklet form. The same is true of cartoons, poems, and children's stories.

If you publish a major work, perhaps you can reprint it in popular and shortened form.

In any case, keep getting mileage out of your writing. This book is itself a rewriting and expanding of two earlier paperbacks!

18

WHAT THE EDITORS WANT

You are a Christian, or you never would have read thus far. Presumably you go to church. As you enter the door, the usher offers you a bulletin. Look carefully at that bulletin. If it is like most church bulletins, it has some empty space; quite possibly the whole back page is blank.

At home in your file is a poem, a rhyme, a devotional thought that has come to you some time in the past. Why not offer it to your pastor and suggest it be printed in the bulletin? Two weeks later offer the pastor something else, perhaps of an inspirational or evangelistic nature. In time you may become a regular contributor. People will tell you how much they appreciate your writing.

Be sure to sign your name to what you submit. Why is that important? Because God gave you that name, and expects you to use it for his glory. God wants to establish you as a professional writer, and he can't do it without your name. Editors will build on your name. Use your own name consistently; only when others might be hurt by your writing is a pen name advisable.

Having proved you can break into print in the church bulletin, you may now think of moving up. Your church may be part of a denomination or an association that has regional and state papers. You can become a correspondent for them. Send in news items, interviews, and reports of speeches. You will soon be receiving assignments from the editor who finds you can be counted on for good, dependable copy.

Join a writers' group, attend a writers' conference, and begin to make friends with people in the writing and editing profession. Rearrange your house or apartment to provide better writing facilities for yourself. You are on your way! Now you set your cap for a national magazine.

Through a friend, you have met somebody really important, and have been promised an interview. You write a query letter, or better, you telephone one of the editors you met at a writers' workshop. You receive a positive response—but no promises. You make the appointment, get the story, write it up, and submit it. It comes back with a personal note of regret. You contact the editor and ask what was wrong with your story. He tells you. He also suggests that you send it to a different magazine. You start over with another query letter. Again a positive response. You send the interview and receive in reply a suggestion for rewriting, with some added information. You get the information, resubmit, and it is accepted. Hallelujah!

Once you are published by an editor, you will find it easier to submit a second article; in fact, the editor may call on you for an assignment. But don't sit around and wait. One of the best approaches to a magazine editor is by way of the calendar, for the editor is acutely calendar-conscious and can never find enough good material on Christmas and Easter. But if the periodical appears monthly, the editor is also open to suggestions for timely articles on other important dates: Pentecost, Reformation Day, the Fourth of July, Labor Day, back-to-school, Thanksgiving, the beginning of Lent, Valentine's Day, and so on. The editor is also aware of centenary observances, and bicentennials, to say nothing of the year 2000 coming up!

Remember that the editor is only a lens for the reader, a front for the market. The real audience we want to reach is in the homes and buildings to which the magazine is delivered. The editor knows the readership, is familiar with its reading tastes. When he scans our material, it is with that audience in view. Will this article evoke a favorable response? He cannot afford too many wrong guesses. Walk a few minutes in the editor's moccasins, and it may do something for your writing.

After the beginning writer, who so often is a woman, has proved her worth and skill in the magazine field (and not before), she can consider herself qualified to try for the book market. Let me share with you a particular problem faced by book editors. Each season—usually twice a year—they have a book list of new offerings to prepare, and they want it to be a winner. In a highly competitive field, the list must be balanced. It must carry some outstanding names, and of course the staple items. But it also needs some new and fresh products that will create excitement in the trade. Thus the aggressive book publisher is looking for a "discovery," for a new name that will prove to be a phenomenon, perhaps even a "bestseller." (Any book that sells 50,000 copies is considered in the Christian market a "best-seller.") If the editor finds a book by a new author that will catch people's attention, his list is made for the season.

That is your book! Many young authors do not realize that while they are looking for markets, the publisher is looking for them. As soon as he is convinced that they have what he wants, he will sign them up. Look at Mrs. Smith, who lives on the south 40 near Hudson, South Dakota. She is banging away at her manual typewriter on the kitchen table, producing something interesting about living the Christian life on a farm in today's world, but she doesn't know where to send it. And here is Editor Jones sitting in his office in New York or Chicago or Grand Rapids, scratching his head and saying, "Wouldn't it be great if we could get something about the gospel from a down-to-earth farmer with a sense of humor?"

Inexperienced writers often fail to take a sensible approach to the editor or publisher. They place him on a pedestal, or on the top floor of a skyscraper on the East Coast. They need to see the editor as one who is constantly looking for fresh talent, hoping that the next writer he meets will fill his need.

I have found that editors are looking for writers who are aware of the times in which they live and who consistently write in the modern vein. They want material that is alive, that pulses with a feeling that "you know where you are." They want Christ in the marketplace. They want material that appeals to their younger readers, that reflects a zestful frame of mind, that avoids clichés, and that takes the reader right into the presence of the Lord.

Now we come to the book itself: what will it say? What is the author's rationale or reason for bringing a book into existence? Is the manuscript just an extension of one's personal ego? If it is, I can guarantee that no publisher of integrity will be interested in it. The basic premise of a book worth publishing can be stated in one sentence. Even before the author sits down to draw up a rough outline, a thought seed should be sprouting in his or her mind.

Once the writer is able to state simply and clearly the idea for a book, the subject should be approached from different perspectives. That is to say, one should be able to develop categories and components. After some study, being careful to avoid duplicating what has already been written in the field, the author can work out a table of contents that contains the outline of the book. He or she then should prepare a sample chapter, or even a few pages, and start making contacts.

Don't write the book and then go looking for a publisher. New writers, particularly, should be in close contact with an editor who believes in them and can give them guidance. The editor knows the market, the readership, and what will sell. Editors must be listened to. I once took a table of contents and a few sample pages of a proposed book to an editor and sat in his office while he went through the copy. Within 15 minutes the deal was closed. However, I did not consult him during the writing of the book. The result was that I had to do it over again. On the rewrite I submitted it two chapters at a time and begged for counsel.

Now let's assume that you are acquainted with an editor. I suggest you impose on that person! For an editor to go to lunch with an author is standard operating procedure; it happens every day. Has it happened to you? I remember with amusement a writer who attended one of our schools in Britain, and then wrote a jingle that went:

> I write, rewrite, and write again.
> I do my best, but here's the crunch:
> How can I afford to take
> Fifty editors out to lunch?

We need not "take out" 50 editors; we want only the editor in whom we are interested and in whose periodical we would like to be published. In a social situation presumably we will make some headway. If the editor doesn't know us as a person already, things will be different from this point on. No longer are we a faceless, unsolicited author. We may be on our way to becoming one of the house writers.

I leave you with this thought: the editor is not going around with pockets filled with rejection slips. Would you like to know what is really in those pockets? Contracts! That's enough to send any aspiring Christian writer to prayer—and to work.

NOTES

1. From John Bunyan, *Pilgrim's Progress.*
2. From Luther's Preface to the Epistle to the Romans.
3. Allport, *Personality: A Psychological Interpretation* (London: Constable, 1949), p. 226.
4. Emil Brunner, *The Divine Imperative* (London: Lutterworth, 1949), p. 259.
5. From *Decision Magazine* (July 1973). Used by permission of Dr. John A. Huffman Jr.
6. *Life,* (Easter, 1956).
7. Sherwood E. Wirt and Ruth McKinney, *You Can Tell the World* (Nashville: Thomas Nelson, 1977), pp. 121-127. Used by permission of Ruth McKinney.

APPENDIX: TOOLS FOR THE PROFESSIONAL CHRISTIAN WRITER

Essential equipment

Desk with drawers; straight chair, office type
Typewriter desk
Electric typewriter or word processor
Proper lighting
Steel filing cabinet; supply cabinet
Desk tools: stapler, staple remover, clips, scissors, calendar, etc.
Ream of good quality 8½"x11" paper
Conveniently located bookshelves
Wastebasket
Tape recorder and blank cassettes

Optional equipment

Clock; telephone; copying machine; postage weighing machine; numbering machine

Literary tools

Two dictionaries: one small, one unabridged
Bibles: NIV, KJV, NEB, NASB, RSV, etc.
One-volume Bible dictionary, e.g., *New Bible Dictionary*, 2nd ed.
One-volume Bible commentary, e.g., *New Bible Commentary Revised*
Synonym finder or Thesaurus, e.g. *The Synonym Finder*
Book of quotations, e.g. *Topical Encyclopedia of Living Quotations*, ed. by Wirt & Beckstrom; or *Oxford Dictionary of Quotations*.
Concordance
Atlas and Bible atlas
Dictionary of the Christian Church
Strunk & White, *Elements of Style*

160 THE MAKING OF A WRITER

Writer's market guide
Encyclopedia
Almanac

Optional literary tools

Geographical dictionary; biographical dictionary; rhyming dictionary
Greek-English New Testament; Hebrew-English Old Testament
Multi-volume Bible commentary
Ancient and modern histories
Poetry anthology
Great Books series

Libraries

Local library; nearby college or university library; Bible college or seminary library; national library